# the book of cool
## VOLUME ONE

THIS IS ONLY THE BEGINNING
www.bookofcool.com

THE BOOK OF COOL™
www.bookofcool.com

Published by Ocelot Productions Ltd, 134 Percival Rd, Enfield, Middlesex, EN1 1QU
Cover design and layout by Dylan Ryan Byrne at BogStandard Ltd.

ISBN 0-9548950-0-2

WRITTEN BY:
FRED REES & DOMINIC SHERIDAN

DESIGNED BY:
DYLAN RYAN BYRNE

This book is designed to be used as an additional guide
to help you master the skills demonstrated in 'the book of cool' DVDs.

DISC 01

■ FRISBEE THROWS . . . . . . . . . . . . . . . . . . . . . . . . . . . . . . . . . . . . . . . . . . . . . . . . 009
■ CASINO SKILLS. . . . . . . . . . . . . . . . . . . . . . . . . . . . . . . . . . . . . . . . . . . . . . . . . . . 035
■ STREET SOCCER MOVES . . . . . . . . . . . . . . . . . . . . . . . . . . . . . . . . . . . . . . . . . 065
■ GUN TRICKS . . . . . . . . . . . . . . . . . . . . . . . . . . . . . . . . . . . . . . . . . . . . . . . . . . . . . . 075
■ STREET BASKETBALL . . . . . . . . . . . . . . . . . . . . . . . . . . . . . . . . . . . . . . . . . . . . . . 091
■ PEN SPINNING . . . . . . . . . . . . . . . . . . . . . . . . . . . . . . . . . . . . . . . . . . . . . . . . . . . . 109

**DISC 02**

■ FREESTYLE FOOTBALL MOVES . . . . . . . . . . . . . . . . . . . . . . . . . . . . . . . . . . . . 121
■ ROPES & WHIPS. . . . . . . . . . . . . . . . . . . . . . . . . . . . . . . . . . . . . . . . . . . . . . . . . . . 139
■ SKATE & BLADE . . . . . . . . . . . . . . . . . . . . . . . . . . . . . . . . . . . . . . . . . . . . . . . . . . . 153
■ CARDS & MAGIC. . . . . . . . . . . . . . . . . . . . . . . . . . . . . . . . . . . . . . . . . . . . . . . . . . . 185
■ JUGGLING . . . . . . . . . . . . . . . . . . . . . . . . . . . . . . . . . . . . . . . . . . . . . . . . . . . . . . . . 191
■ FLATLAND BIKE SKILLS . . . . . . . . . . . . . . . . . . . . . . . . . . . . . . . . . . . . . . . . . . . . 199

**DISC 03**

■ RUGBY KICKS . . . . . . . . . . . . . . . . . . . . . . . . . . . . . . . . . . . . . . . . . . . . . . . . . . . . . 213
■ GOLF TRICKS & SKILLS . . . . . . . . . . . . . . . . . . . . . . . . . . . . . . . . . . . . . . . . . . . . 227
■ BAR FLAIRING. . . . . . . . . . . . . . . . . . . . . . . . . . . . . . . . . . . . . . . . . . . . . . . . . . . . . 237
□ POOL SHOTS . . . . . . . . . . . . . . . . . . . . . . . . . . . . . . . . . . . . . . . . . . . . . . . . . . . . . . 265
■ FOOTBAG MOVES . . . . . . . . . . . . . . . . . . . . . . . . . . . . . . . . . . . . . . . . . . . . . . . . . 293
■ MORE . . . . . . . . . . . . . . . . . . . . . . . . . . . . . . . . . . . . . . . . . . . . . . . . . . . . . . . . . . . . . 305

contents

"One thousand days to learn, ten thousand days to refine."
MIYAMOTO MUSASHI
LEGENDARY SAMURAI, REMEMBERED AS A KENSHI OR SWORD SAINT
MUSASHI, JAPAN

"You can learn this in one day, guaranteed!"
CHRISTIAN DELPECH
8 x WORLD BAR FLAIRING CHAMPION
BUENOS AIRES, ARGENTINA

# WARNING!

- The people featured in this product are all experts and highly skilled in their chosen fields.

- Some of the activities featured in 'the book of cool' can be hazardous.

- Where appropriate you must wear all recommended protective clothing and equipment.

- Master the basics before attempting any advanced skills.

- Always practise the skills featured in a safe environment.

- If you have any doubt about your ability to attempt a skill safely, do not attempt it, seek tuition from a professional or recognised expert in the field!

- Always consider your safety and the safety of others around you.

# FRISBEE™

## TOM LEITNER
SANTA CRUZ, CALIFORNIA, USA

**BACKHAND** THROW .010

**FLICK** .012

**THUMBER** .014

OVERHAND **WRIST FLIP** .016

**HAMMER** .018

**HOOK** THUMBER .020

**AIR** BOUNCE .022

**HELICOPTER** .024

**CATCHES** .026

**TIPPING** & **SPINNING** .028

**AIR BRUSHING** & **BODY ROLLS** .032

# BACKHAND THROW
## PART 01

**1** Grab the disc like you are shaking somebody's hand

**2** Index finger on rim or curled underneath for more distance

Bottom three fingers underneath

Thumb on top

**3** Stand sideways to your target

Rotate forearm to make disc level

Push off front leg for more distance

Keep eyes on target - if there's forward movement after throw make sure it is towards the target

Snap hand back to create more Zs (spin)

# FLICK
## PART 01

1 Make peace sign - two fingers inside

2 Thumb on top - two fingers curled into palm

Power of flick comes from this finger

3 Keep outside edge down to level out flight of disc

Lean back for more power

Flick hand back after throw to increase speed and spin

# THUMBER

## THE GRIP

**1** Thumb on inside

**2** Four fingers on top

Keep back of frisbee tilted down

**3** Lean back to help keep front edge up

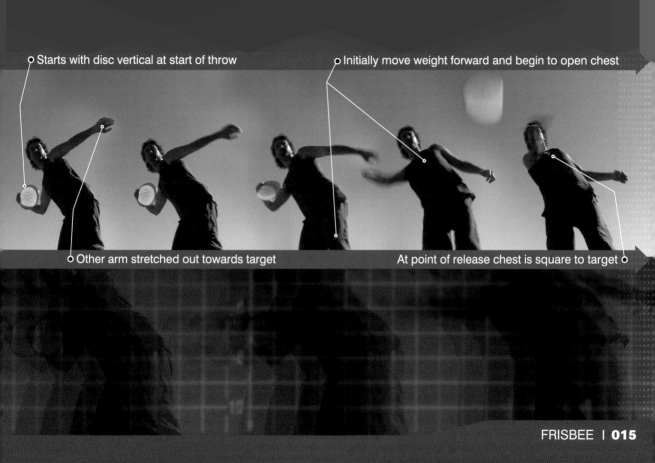

Starts with disc vertical at start of throw

Initially move weight forward and begin to open chest

Other arm stretched out towards target

At point of release chest is square to target

FRISBEE | **015**

Four fingers on top, index along edge

Thumb on inside against rim

Wrist angled back

○ At back of throw disc is behind body - arm is straight - side-on to target

○ As throw begins, weight moves onto front foot, shoulders start to open

Start wrist flick

Disc flat at point of release

Body angled to left to help level up disc

Hand flicks back after release to create spin - chest points just to right of target

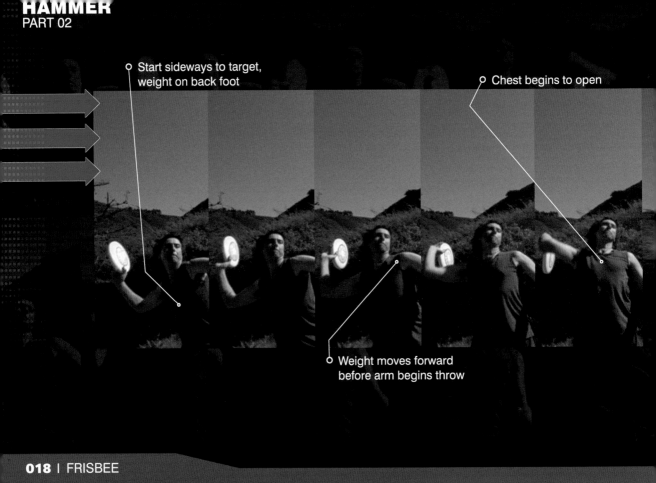

# HAMMER
PART 02

Start sideways to target, weight on back foot

Chest begins to open

Weight moves forward before arm begins throw

End with chest square to target

Wind up with shoulders twisting against hips

At point of full wind up, back is nearly turned to face target

Thumb on inside of rim, four fingers outside - make a fist. Stand sideways to your target

At point of release, shoulders side-on to target. Use thumb for more snap

After release, shoulders open up to face target (amount depends on initial wind up)

# AIR BOUNCE

1 Normal backhand grip side on to target

2 Raise front foot as disc is pulled back

3 At top of backswing leg is also at top of lift - disc at 45% angle to ground

4 Leg drops to create initial momentum

5 Leg pushes against ground for extra speed

6 Tilt front edge up at last second - knees bend bringing disc closer to ground

7 At point of release disc just above knee level - arm is nearly straight

8 Chest turned towards target - follow through behind back

# HELICOPTER

Non-throwing arm points towards target

Chest angled back against hips, facing towards the sky. Disc parallel to chest so chest to sky = flat disc. Throwing arm begins movement

Sideways to target

Chest leans forward

Disc upside down for maximum rotation

Throw begins with weight moving to back foot and chest beginning to open. Throwing arm does not move but is pulled by upper body movement

Same grip as overhand wrist flick
Thumb on inside four fingers on top

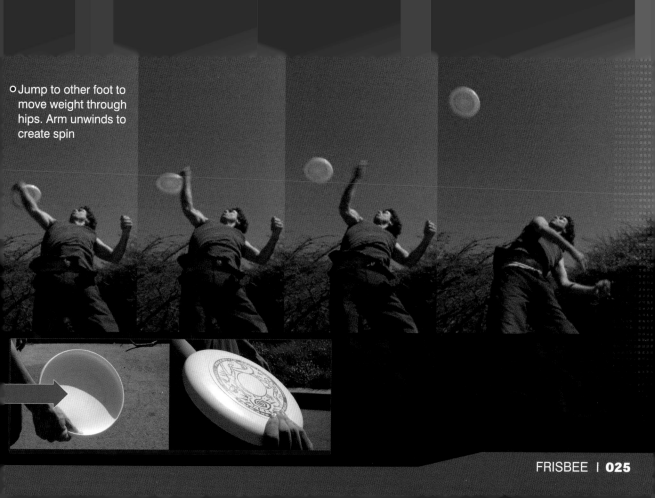

Jump to other foot to move weight through hips. Arm unwinds to create spin

# CATCHES

o Gitis

o Under the Leg

• Behind the Back

• Behind the Head

• Flamingo

# TIPPING

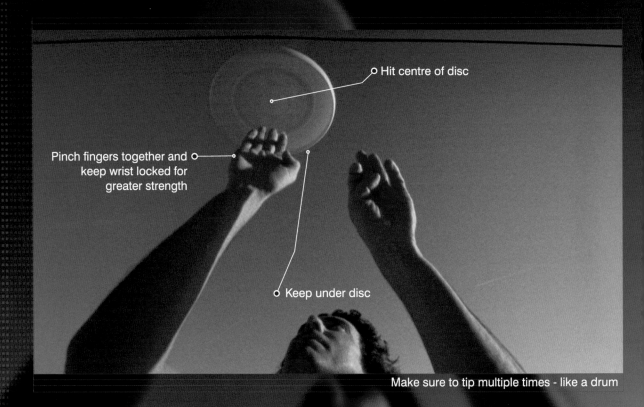

Hit centre of disc

Pinch fingers together and keep wrist locked for greater strength

Keep under disc

Make sure to tip multiple times - like a drum

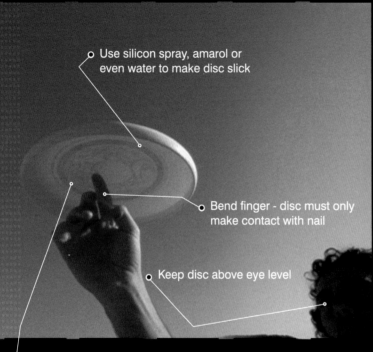

Use silicon spray, amarol or even water to make disc slick

Bend finger - disc must only make contact with nail

Keep disc above eye level

Rotate hand with movement of disc
Like swirling a glass of wine

Grip disc in front of you, hands on either side

Pull one hand towards you to wind up disc

Move disc to your side and down to create more space for spin creation

\* Use fake plastic nail for
more spinning control
and rim delays

Average wind

Strong wind

Hit disc in direction it is spinning

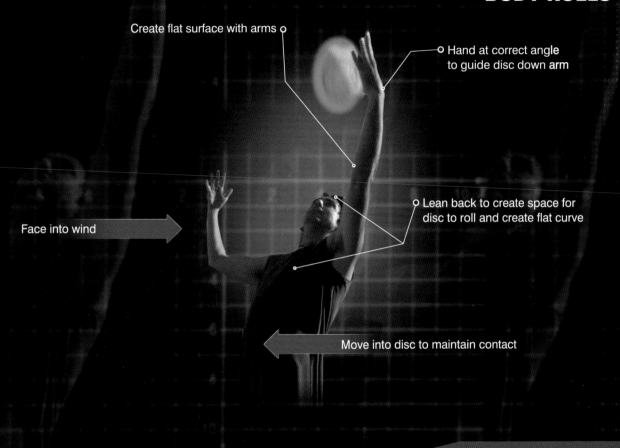

Create flat surface with arms

Hand at correct angle to guide disc down arm

Lean back to create space for disc to roll and create flat curve

Face into wind

Move into disc to maintain contact

# CASINO&CARDS

## GEORGE JOSEPH
LAS VEGAS, USA

GAMBLING

036 **SHUFFLING**

038 **DEALING**

040 **TURN** & **PITCH**

041 **POP** & **PITCH**

042 **FLICK** & **PITCH**

044 **TEXAS HOLD 'EM** - BASIC RULES

045 STUD **POP** & **LAY**

046 **CHECK** HANDLING

047 **THUMB** BUSTING

048 **CHECK** FLOURISH

050 **COIN** ROLL

CUTS, SHUFFLES & FLOURISHES

**RIBBON** SPREAD .052

**ONE**-HANDED **CUT** .054

**FARO SHUFFLE** WITH **BUTT FLOURISH** .056

**RUSSIAN** SHUFFLE .058

**BUTTERFLY** SHUFFLE .059

**NIAGARA FALLS** SHUFFLE .060

**FANS** .062

**1** Practise position

**2**

**3** Appox. 1 inch high
Master gentle riffle

**4** Approx. 1/2 inch
Lift - Turn - Riffle

**5** Push - Straighten

**6** Finish

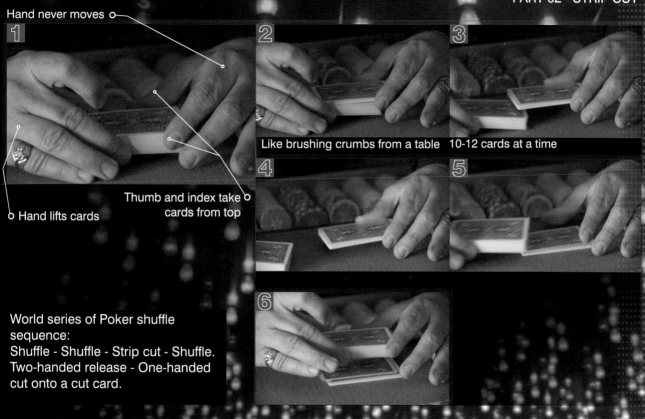

Hand never moves

Hand lifts cards

Thumb and index take cards from top

1

2 Like brushing crumbs from a table

3 10-12 cards at a time

4

5

6

World series of Poker shuffle sequence:
Shuffle - Shuffle - Strip cut - Shuffle.
Two-handed release - One-handed cut onto a cut card.

# DEALING
## PART 01

Thumb across side
of deck when at rest

Thumb pivots off top card
against base of palm

**1** DEALER/MECHANIC'S GRIP

**2**

**3**

Corner separated by
index and middle finger

Like you're making a fake gun

Corner in fat of heel of palm

PITCHING

○ When card clears deck, set on middle finger of right hand with card resting on back edge of index finger – thumb on top

○ Middle finger flicks out card. As if you're flicking somebody in the head. Momentum comes from middle finger not index. Card spins to target

Turn body to change pitch direction. Practise with handcuffs or a rubber band.
Practise pitching into a hat - pitch straight. For Texas Hold 'Em keep deck low to table to prevent showing cards.

Sound of snap comes from card flicking against side of deck

Thumb pushes card forward of
deck - approx. 1/4 inch o—

1

2

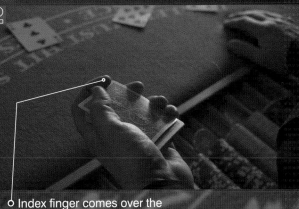

o Index finger comes over the
front of card

3

o Index finger pops up card

o Thumb clears side of deck

NOTE:

Place card on table with other hand.

Reposition cards against body if
grip is lost - for ease push card
forward and away diagonally from
deck in order to create more space.

# FLICK & PITCH
## PART 01

**The Grip**
Little finger above back
of cards for leverage

Thumb pushes card back and then raises
at front before release

Thumb pushes card
back towards little finger

Thumb is on top edge of card
not against the corner

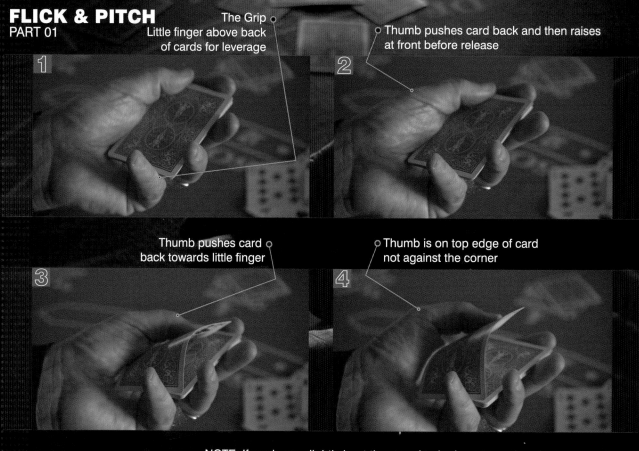

NOTE: If cards are slightly bent they need to be bent towards palm to ease release.

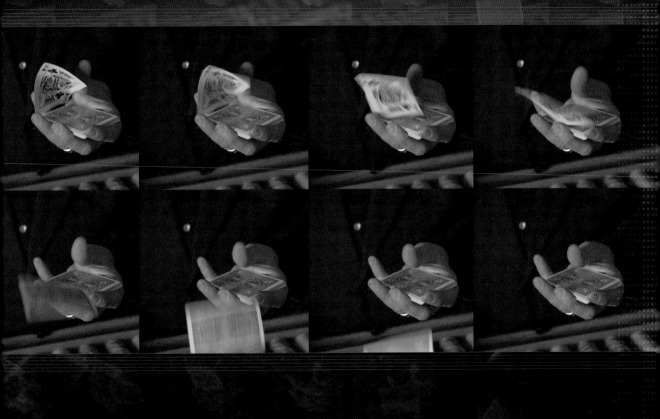

# TEXAS HOLD 'EM · BASIC RULES

A hand in Texas Hold 'Em is made up of five cards:
The cards a player uses to make up his hand can be any combination of his hole cards and the communal cards on the table. It is possible to have a hand that consists solely of the communal cards which does not utilize either of the hole cards a player has been dealt.

## ORDER OF PLAY:

- Each player dealt two cards face down - "Hole cards"
- Round of betting
- Three communal cards dealt face up on table - "The Flop"
- Round of betting
- One communal card dealt face up on table - "4th Street"
- Round of betting
- One communal card dealt face up on table - "The River"
- Round of betting

- Players left in game show cards - best hand wins.

An unbeatable hand is called "The Nuts".
A hand with a pair of aces and a pair of eights is known as the "Dead Man's Hand" because Wild Bill Hickock was holding these cards when he was shot through the back and killed.

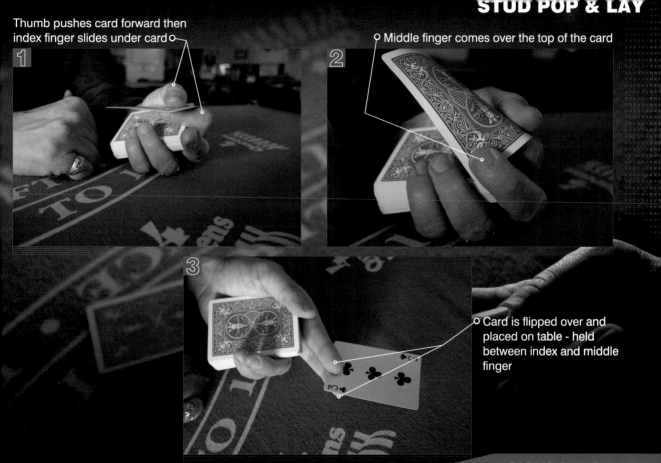

1. Thumb pushes card forward then index finger slides under card

2. Middle finger comes over the top of the card

3. Card is flipped over and placed on table - held between index and middle finger

# CHECK HANDLING

### Initial grip for drop cutting

**1**

### Separate checks with index finger

**2**

### Thumb and little finger act as hinge behind checks

**3**

### Index cuts back across top of checks and hand moves back to create new stack

**4**

Size in sideways - thumb cuts chips - back three fingers push stack

# CHECK FLOURISH

Middle finger sets in between chips

These digits hold chips on either side

Middle finger lifts chips, then drops bottom check as side digits massage them together.

# COIN ROLL

Thumb slides coin over index finger

Coin slides under edge of middle finger

Middle finger drops down lifting coin over

Index finger rises to help move coin

Middle finger already raised

Ring finger rises

Coin will then slide under edge of ring finger

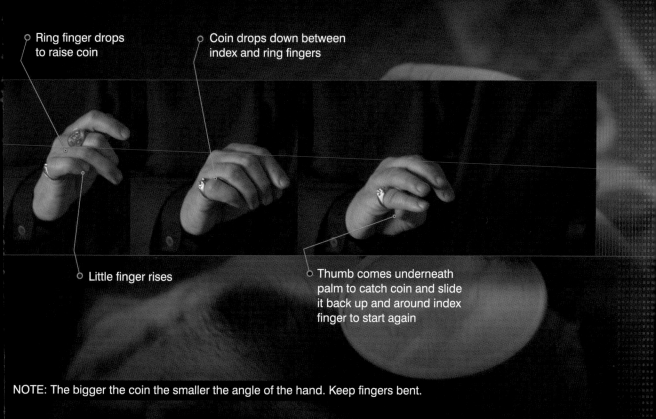

Ring finger drops to raise coin

Coin drops down between index and ring fingers

Little finger rises

Thumb comes underneath palm to catch coin and slide it back up and around index finger to start again

NOTE: The bigger the coin the smaller the angle of the hand. Keep fingers bent.

# RIBBON SPREAD
## PART 01 - THE GRIP

1

Pressure from index determines length of
spread. More pressure less spread

2

Fingers are nearly flat on top of cards.
At end of spread, hand nearly flat on table

3

Lift card until perpendicular to felt then
give it a push. More push more speed

4

Use fingers or a joker to split the ribbon

## 1 The Grip

## 2

Cut deck with thumb

Index releases

## 3

Index finger pushes back towards you not up

## 4

Hand opens slighlty to let cards fall.
Thumb pushes bottom half onto top

# FARO SHUFFLE WITH BUTT FLOURISH

Push gently together - open slightly at the front and lift

Move one half of deck
slightly forward to
help interlace

For flourish lift cards with fingers
underneath deck, place thumbs
above overlapping top cards

LIFT - BEND - PUSH CARDS TOGETHER

5

6

4

NOTE:
Eight perfect Faro shuffles return
the deck to its original order!

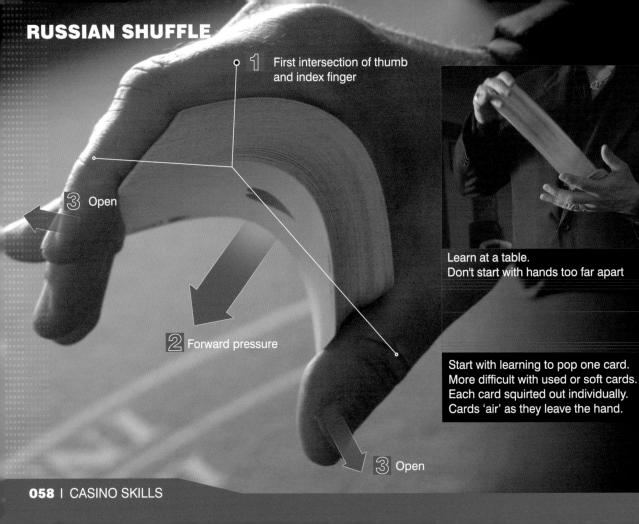

# RUSSIAN SHUFFLE

1 First intersection of thumb and index finger

3 Open

2 Forward pressure

3 Open

Learn at a table.
Don't start with hands too far apart

Start with learning to pop one card.
More difficult with used or soft cards.
Each card squirted out individually.
Cards 'air' as they leave the hand.

**1** Riffle with thumb to split deck

Grip for butterfly - "dealer's grip"

**2** Each half of deck nestles in crotch of thumb

**3** Riffle back of cards with little finger.
Master this before attempting shuffle

Bring back of cards together, riffle with little fingers.
Cards will interlace

**4** Note, only thumb, index & little fingers
in contact with cards at point of shuffle.
Middle fingers out of the way

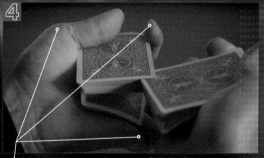

Same grip as Russian shuffle - insert air in between cards - gently release grip starting from fingertips

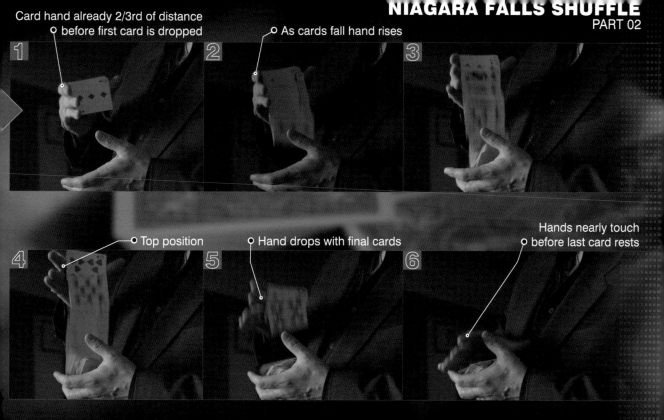

Card hand already 2/3rd of distance
before first card is dropped

As cards fall hand rises

Top position

Hand drops with final cards

Hands nearly touch
before last card rests

NOTE:
Initially practise with hands close together.

# FANS

Thumb just to left of centre

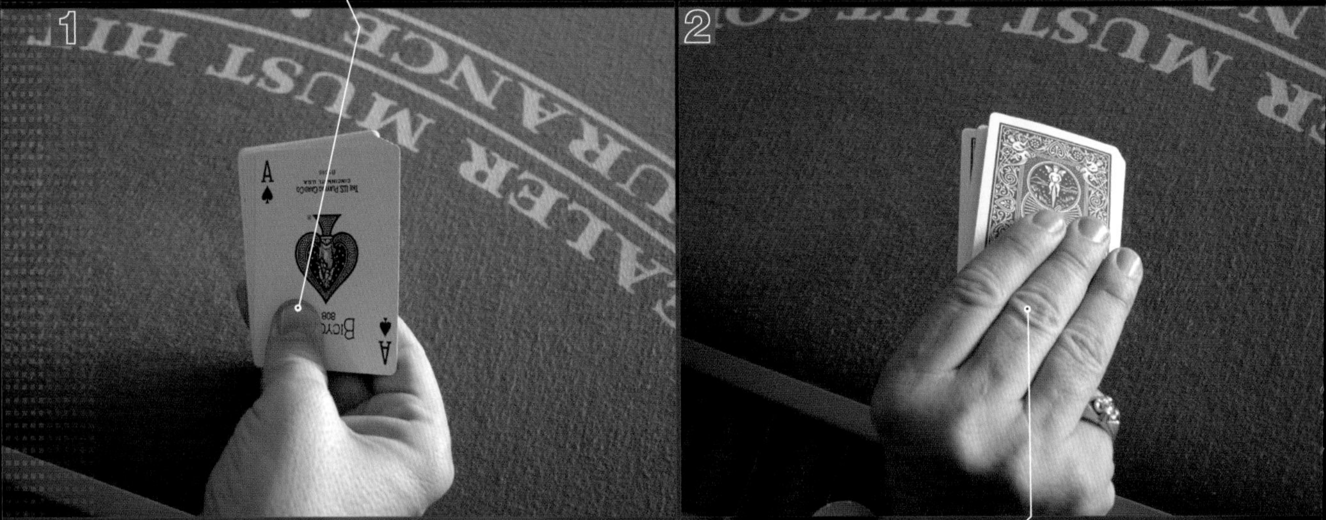

Three fingers on back of card

**3** Turn hand and twist fingers against thumb to fan

**4** Practise first with two cards then three then four, until 26 in each hand

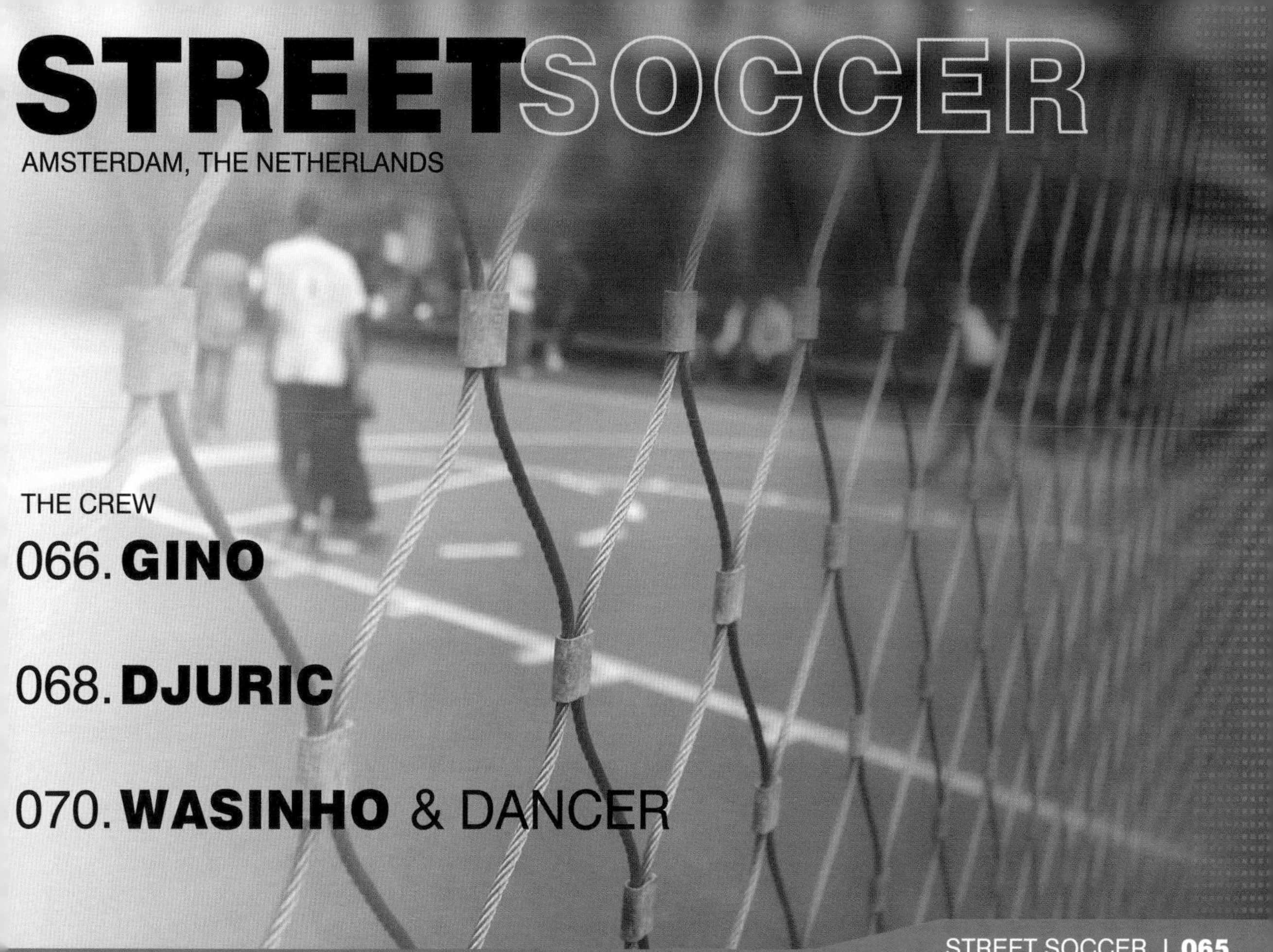

# STREETSOCCER

AMSTERDAM, THE NETHERLANDS

THE CREW

066. **GINO**

068. **DJURIC**

070. **WASINHO** & DANCER

Foot drags ball back
onto right foot

Right body turn

Right foot catches ball against back of left foot

Foot drags ball up the back of left thigh

Left heel kicks ball back into the air

# Djoric
## THE LOW DOWN

DJURIC

**1**

Roll ball forward with the top of right foot

Right foot steps forward over ball, left knee bends

Ball hits knee and bounces right

Right foot then hits back up to your left

Left foot grabs ball

Right foot on top of ball

**3**

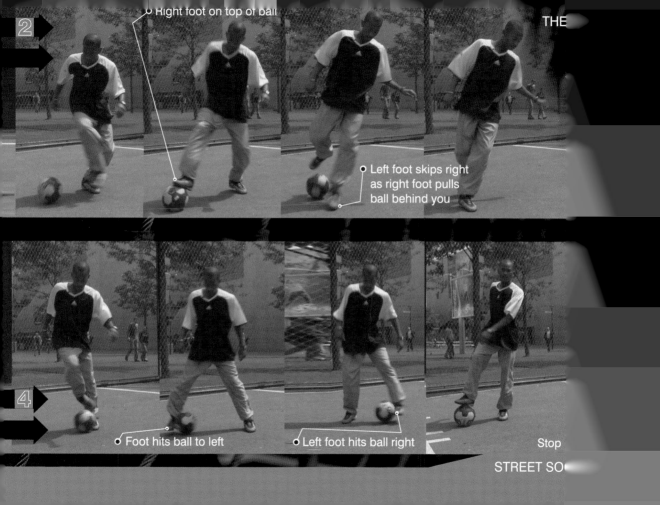

Right foot on top of ball

THE

Left foot skips right
as right foot pulls
ball behind you

Foot hits ball to left

Left foot hits ball right

Stop

STREET SO

DANCER

Pull ball slowly back behind you and to the right

Watch out for him!

WASINHO

REET SOCCER

1st circle

Three circles in total then catch ball with tip of foot

Pull ball back between legs

The defenders are Jokers - and you're the Man!

# WASINHO
## THE SNAKE

○ The defender will go crazy
○ Poisonous like a snake

DANCER

# WATCH OUT!

• Peace out

STREET SOCCER | **073**

# GUNTRICKS

## HOWARD DARBY
CALGARY, CANADA

WARNING! .076

DRAW .077

FAST DRAW .078

OVER THE TOP FLIP .079

GUN SPINNING .080

FLAT SPINS .081

BACK SPIN DRAW .082

SHOULDER ROLL .084

CURLY BILL SPIN .086

BACK SPIN HOLSTERING .087

FORWARD SPIN HOLSTERING .088

ROUND & IN THE BACK .089

# WARNING!

Never use a real gun!
In some countries, the ownership or possession of a gun, real or fake, is against the law. You should always obey the laws of your country.

Only carry out the tricks shown in this book with replica or plastic guns.

The book of cool does not condone the use of guns in any way and if you have a gun, even if it is within the law, get rid of it. You don't need it!

# DRAW

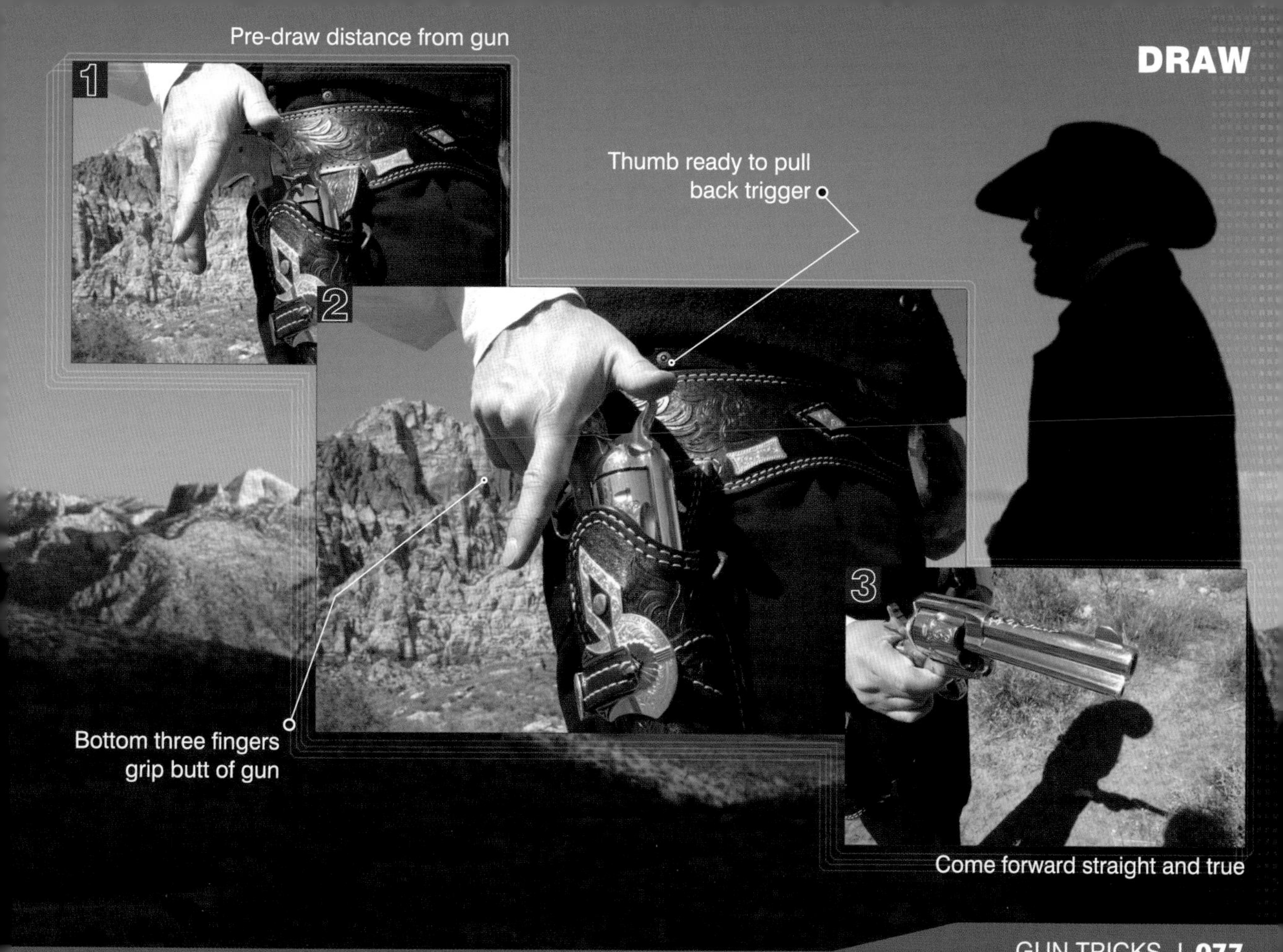

Pre-draw distance from gun
1
2
Thumb ready to pull back trigger
Bottom three fingers grip butt of gun
3
Come forward straight and true

# THE FAST DRAW

**1** Pull back hammer as you start the draw

Howard Darby Fast Draw Speed 0.256 Sec.
Currently the 'Fastest Gun Alive'

**3** Pull trigger as barrel clears holster

**2** Angled body position
- all one movement

NOTE:
Fast draw holsters for competitions have steel lining
and a solid bottom to prevent accidents when the
gun is fired too early.

Lift gun with trigger finger only

Fast arched movement

Pull back trigger at this point

# GUN SPINNING

**1** Keep fingers and thumb out of the way

Keep trigger finger crooked

**2**

Move hand up and down to create movement - if single spin pull hand slightly back towards body. The faster the spin the less movement required.

**NOTE:**
If you're finding it difficult to straighten fingers and keep them out of the way of the spin then try gentle finger massage/finger yoga.

Strong flick to create spin

Hand drops and rises

Pushes away and pulls back as gun spins

## UNDER FLAT SPIN

Start with gun low and close to body

Up and away from hip
Release gun at this point

As arm straightens pull back and down towards body

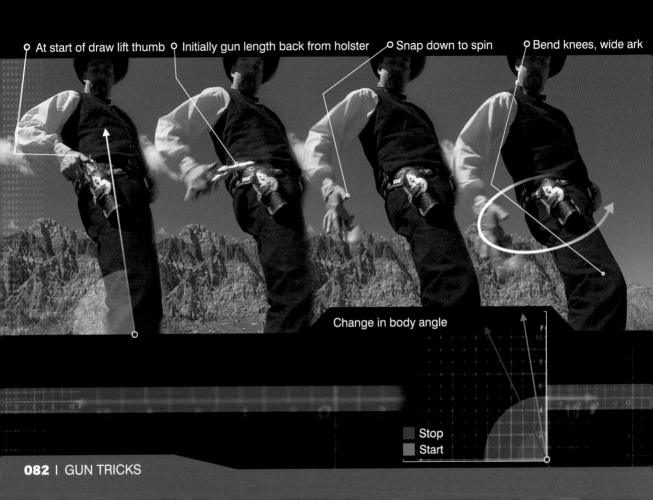

At start of draw lift thumb

Initially gun length back from holster

Snap down to spin

Bend knees, wide ark

Change in body angle

Stop
Start

**THE GRIP**

Back three fingers as per basic draw

Finger on trigger to enable spin

# SHOULDER ROLL

1. Strong flick and straight gun o

2. Keep bead on gun as it rolls over shoulder gauge spin speed and angle

3. Slow spinning gun = Lower delayed catch

Move should be one continuous action from frame 1 through to 4

1

2

3

4

5 Once gun comes up pull back trigger

NOTE: Move used by Clint in the film 'Outlaw Josey Wales'.

## SINGLE SPIN

**1** Front of barrel hits front of holster

**2** Snap back and down into holster

## DOUBLE SPIN

**3** First spin at arms length

**4** On 2nd spin pull back towards holster

**5** Again hits front of holster

# FORWARD SPIN HOLSTERING

PRACTISE SLOWLY!

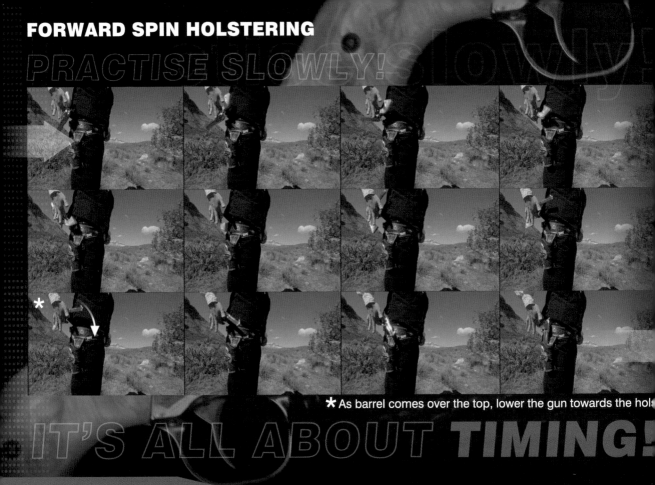

\* As barrel comes over the top, lower the gun towards the holster

IT'S ALL ABOUT TIMING!

When barrel comes over the top of holster drop down and snap in

NOTE: He seems to come higher than he says.  So possibly go over and up rather than round the back and in.

# STREETBALL

STREET BASKETBALL ASSOCIATION
WASHINGTON DC, USA

THE CREW

092. **PAT-**'DA-ROCK' **ROBINSON**

096. **ANDRE** 'SILK' **POOLE**

099. **BRIAN** 'X-RATED' **MILLS**

102. **HUGH** 'BABY SHAQ' **JONES**

104. **PEP** 'HARLEM WORLD' **TYSON**

106. **RASHID** '7 & SOME CHANGE' **BYRD**

# PAT-'DA-ROCK' ROBINSON
## ARM WAVE

Keep eyes on ball at all times

Arm moves/bends with ball

Ball lands on shoulder or just below

Ball rolls over top of hand

# PAT-'DA-ROCK' ROBINSON
## ARM WAVE

Hand catches/grabs hold of ball

Throw needs to be high enough to roll onto shoulder

# PAT-'DA-ROCK' ROBINSON
## FINGER SPIN

Thumb and other fingers together to help support index finger

Finger in centre of ball

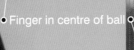

- Use arm, finger and thumb to spin ball - ball should spin in to out.
- Less speed is easier for a short spin when learning but to really get it spinning the throw must be fast.
- Throw the ball up in air, above head height, in order to clearly see the calm centre spot of the spinning ball.
- The more central the axis of the spin as caused by the throw the easier it is - go for level spins.
- Skim ball with other hand to increase speed - if hitting away from you ball must be spinning in to out.

Concentrate on the ball

Ball on fingertips

Thumb bent into palm, four fingers cuffed

Contact with outside top of fingers

...ike you're waving to somebody - "Hey what's up?"

Contact with inside top of fingers

# ANDRE 'SILK' POOLE

SILK

# ANDRE 'SILK' POOLE

**HESITATION CROSSOVER**     **HANDS UP**     **360° BOOMERANG**

You gotta rock to your left then go to your right

Make like you're going for a jump shot but your hand never touches the ball

The crew dreamed that robbing a bank might be a better option than this filming lark!

X-RATED

# BRIAN 'X-RATED' MILLS
## THE HYPNOTISER

BABY SHAQ

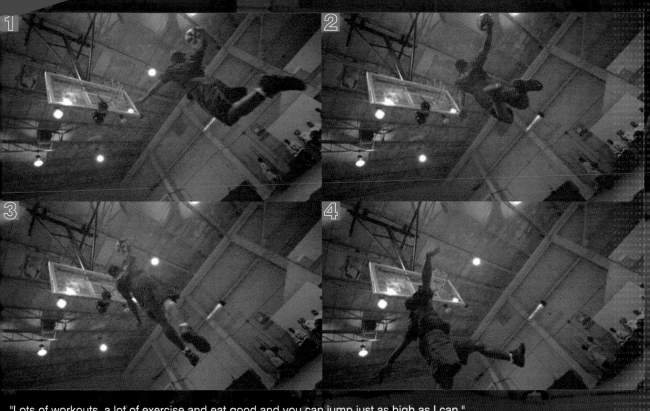

"Lots of workouts, a lot of exercise and eat good and you can jump just as high as I can."
Hugh Jones a.k.a 'Baby Shaq' a.k.a 'Your worst nightmare'

THE Y2K

THE A.I.

# RASHID '7 & SOME CHANGE' BYRD

"Stay outta my Kitchen"

# PEN SPINNING

## DAVID WEIS
AUSTIN, TEXAS, USA

110. **FORWARD** THUMB **SPIN**

114. **REVERSE** THUMB **SPIN**

116. **FAKE REVERSE** THUMB **SPIN**

118. THUMB **SNAP**

Find balance point

Rotate pencil around thumb to start position

# FORWARD THUMB SPIN
## SPINNING BASICS

Pencil at 45°

PUSHING

BLOCKING

CATCHING

Top of hand nearly level to ground

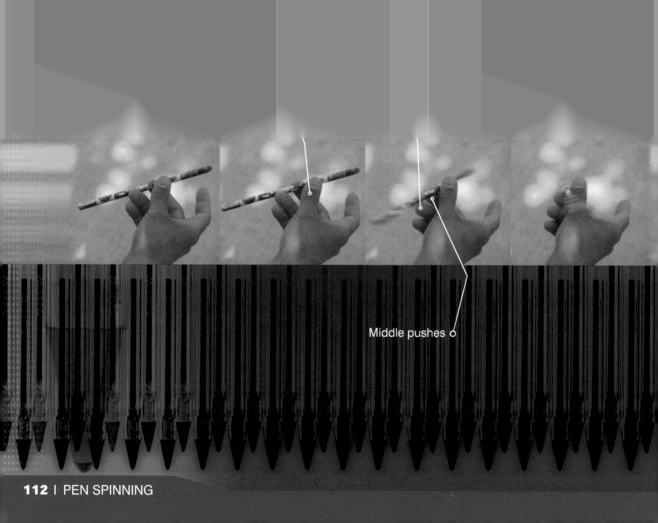

Middle pushes

Hand levels out

Catch begins

Finish

# REVERSE THUMB SPIN

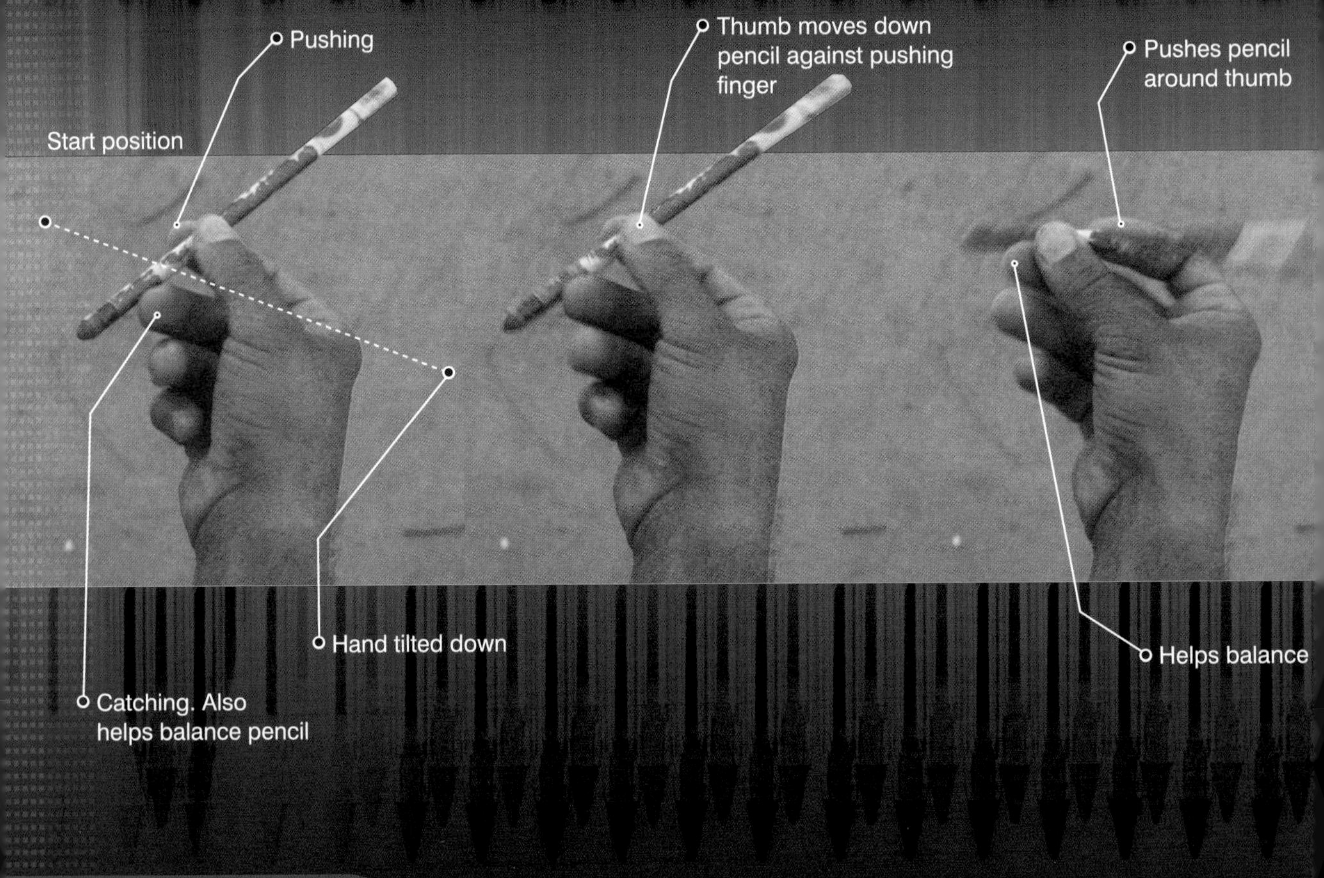

Pushing

Thumb moves down
pencil against pushing
finger

Pushes pencil
around thumb

Start position

Hand tilted down

Helps balance

Catching. Also
helps balance pencil

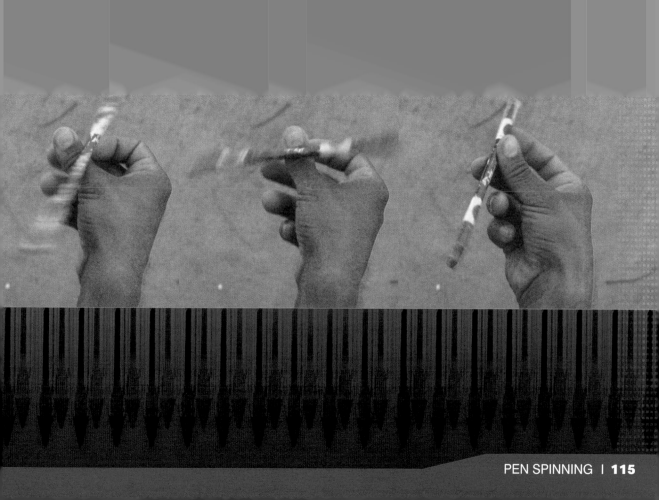

# FAKE REVERSE THUMB SPIN

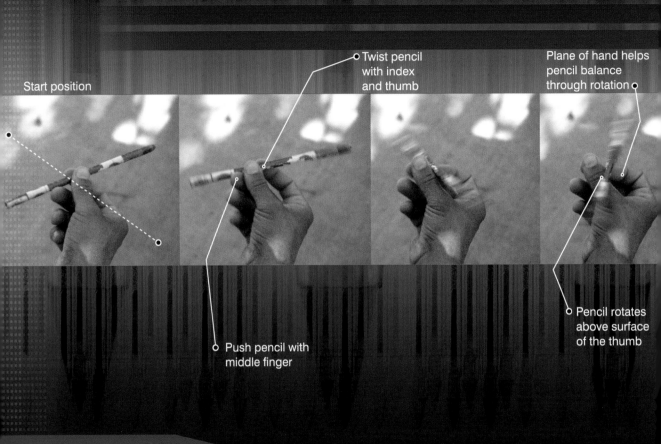

Start position

Twist pencil with index and thumb

Plane of hand helps pencil balance through rotation

Push pencil with middle finger

Pencil rotates above surface of the thumb

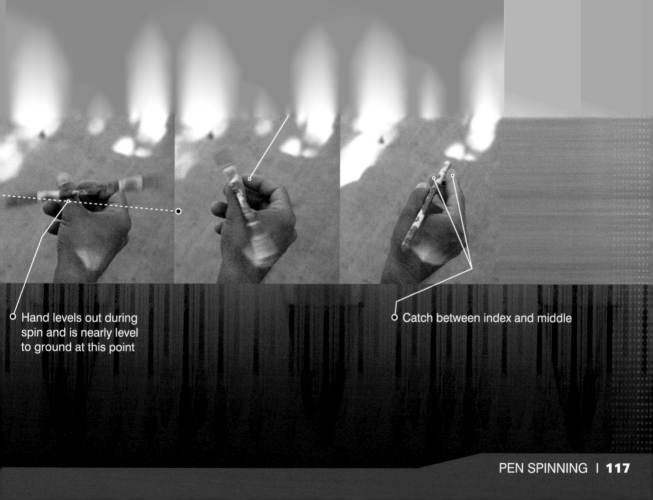

Hand levels out during spin and is nearly level to ground at this point

Catch between index and middle

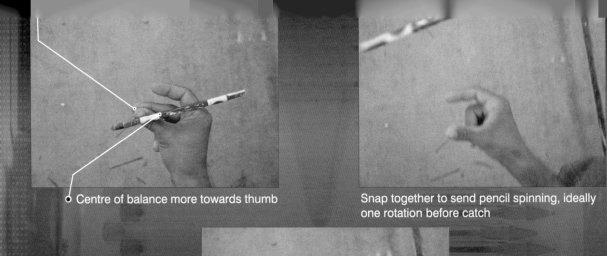

Centre of balance more towards thumb

Snap together to send pencil spinning, ideally one rotation before catch

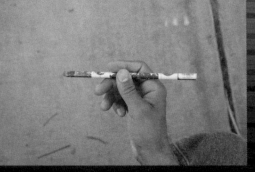

Correct catching position enables other tricks

NOTE:
Can be used on its own before any other pen trick has been learnt - Flick & Catch - 1, 2, 3 spins.
The closer the end of the pencil to the thumb the faster the rotation.

# FOOTBALL

## MR. WOO
SEOUL, SOUTH KOREA

122. **SAYINGS** OF **WOO**

123. THE **CENTRE**

124. **CONTROL**

126. **FLIP** UPS

130. **SUPER** SENSES

132. **USE** YOUR **HEAD**

134. **ROUND** THE **WORLD**

136. **FLYING** KICK

# SAYINGS OF WOO

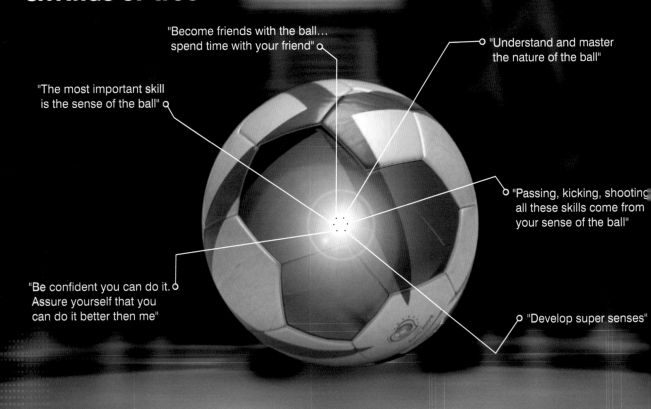

"Become friends with the ball...
spend time with your friend"

"Understand and master
the nature of the ball"

"The most important skill
is the sense of the ball"

"Passing, kicking, shooting
all these skills come from
your sense of the ball"

"Be confident you can do it.
Assure yourself that you
can do it better then me"

"Develop super senses"

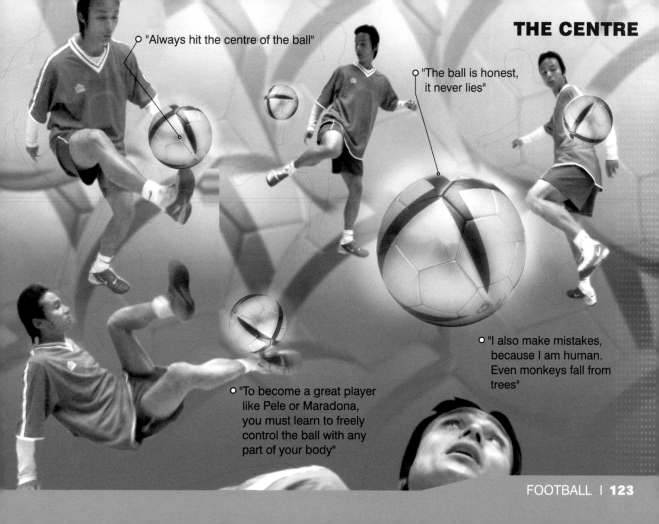

THE CENTRE

"Always hit the centre of the ball"

"The ball is honest, it never lies"

"I also make mistakes, because I am human. Even monkeys fall from trees"

"To become a great player like Pele or Maradona, you must learn to freely control the ball with any part of your body"

Bounce ball no higher than your
knee to maintain balance
and control

Keep the ball below the knee, maintain a steady posture, with your chest over the ball.
Hit the exact centre of the ball and then you will get the most exact balance and posture and achieve a steady rhythm.

# FLIP UPS
## PULL & FLICK

Pull ball back with left foot

As ball comes back right foot skips forward under ball

Pull ball back with right foot

Right foot placed back on ground

As ball reaches left foot,
raise foot to flick ball into the air

# FLIP UPS
## SLAP SAME TIME

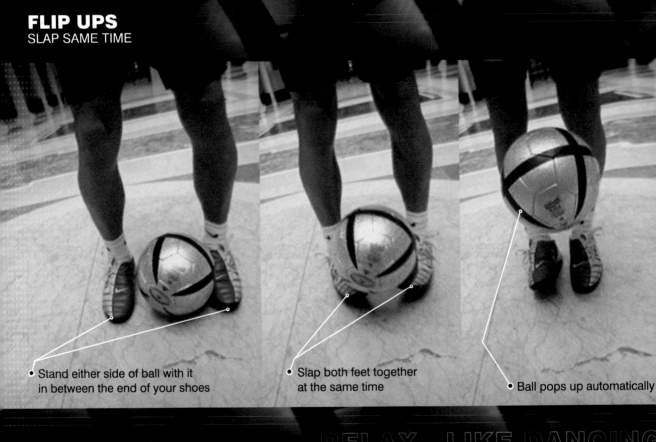

Stand either side of ball with it in between the end of your shoes

Slap both feet together at the same time

Ball pops up automatically

RELAX · LIKE DANCING

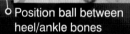

Position ball between heel/ankle bones

Weight shifts to left foot, centre of balance just inside left leg

Right foot pushes ball into left ankle and then rolls it over ankle bone

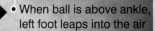

When ball is above ankle, left foot leaps into the air

Ball rolls back down foot and is flicked into the air

# SUPER SENSES

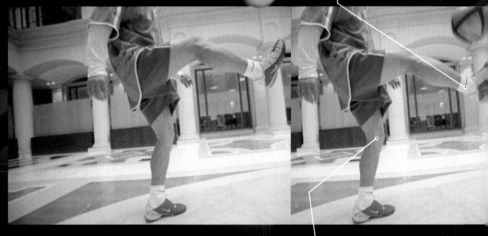

Foot descends at a slightly slower pace then the ball

Knee slightly bent

NOTE:
Become one with the ball.
Super senses will develop as you practise and become one with the ball.
Super sense does not develop overnight...it only comes with constant practice.
When controlling a high ball, train your senses to find the exact centre of the ball.

When centre of ball balanced on foot, bring foot diagonally towards your body

Slow down descent of foo to a gentle stop

The moment you come into contact with the ball, you should relax completel if you put strength into your body the ball will leave.

Use your knees to move your head and header the ball - do not strain with your neck.
you can identify the centre point accurately with your eye and hit it, then the ball is 100% sure to go where you wan

# ROUND THE WORLD

Chest and head towards centre of ball

Take the tension from your body and lift the ball from its central point, as the foot is moving upwards it remains in contact with the ball

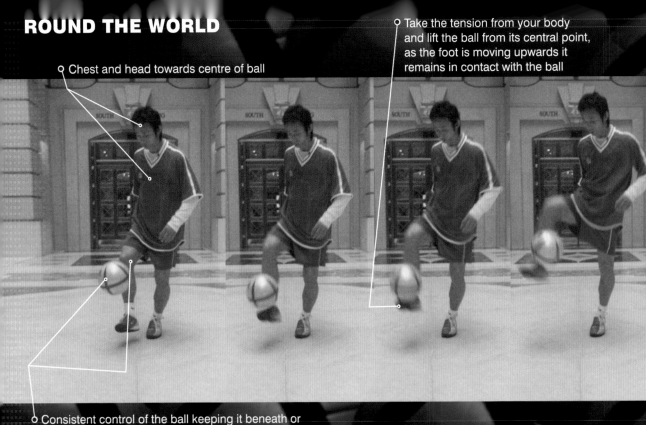

Consistent control of the ball keeping it beneath or level with the knee before attempting move

Swing leg around ball predominantly from the knee not the thigh

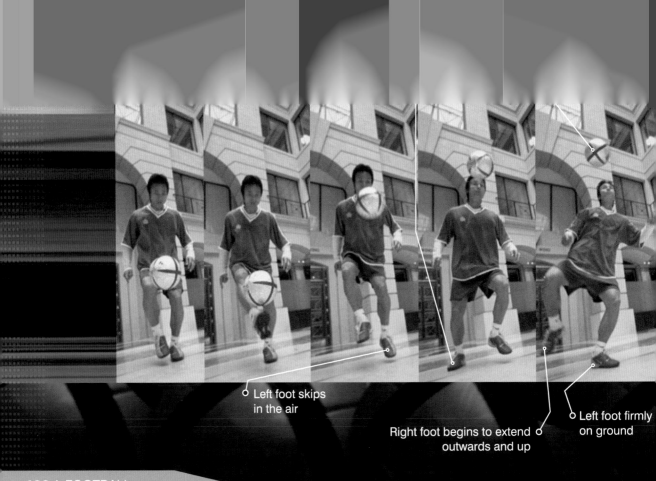

Left foot skips in the air

Right foot begins to extend outwards and up

Left foot firmly on ground

Momentum of leg helps lift body

As ball descends past face left foot leaps from ground to begin kick

Right foot clears over top of ball

"The most important thing is the condition of my body balance."

# ROPES &WHIPS

## VINCE BRUCE
### SARASOTA, FLORIDA, USA

140. **FLAT** SPIN

141. **WEDDING** RING

143. **BUTTERFLY**

144. **OVERHAND** KNOT

146. **FIGURE 8** KNOT

149. **LASSOING**

150. **WHIPS**

# FLAT SPIN

Pull rope through Honda this way

Rope across little finger for easy release

Twist rope between thumb and index finger

NOTE:
Release and spin at same time.
Use arm not wrist. Go slowly.

1 Hand above head

2 Release 'peg' hand as Honda goes behind head

3 Release rope just before hand comes to front

NOTE:
Real slow, like putting on a cloak.
Keep hand above head and in middle of circle.

**1** Honda 1/3rd of way down loop

**2**

Keep loops parallel - two on one side, two on the other.
Move down to connect to other side - not straight across.

# OVERHAND KNOT

**1**

**2** Rope rests on inside of index finger

Flick rope up on inside of hand

**3** Move hand up, flick over and then down. Index finger on top of rope

**4** Rope should rise to initial hand level as it passes through half hitch

# FIGURE 8 KNOT

**1**

**2**

Begin by making same move as overhand but at this point begin to twist wrist outwards

**3**

Hand twists outwards - palm towards the sky

# FIGURE 8 KNOT

**5** Hand then moves over and down

**4** Loop wraps around wrist

**6** Loop snares end of rope

## LASSOING

- Rope goes this way, does not fold back against Honda

As hand reaches front twist wrist to leave palm face up again •

Honda now at bottom of loop •

○ When hand is in back position - palm up

Honda at top of loop •

As hand reaches side of head •
begin wrist turn

Hand stretches towards •
target as lasso released

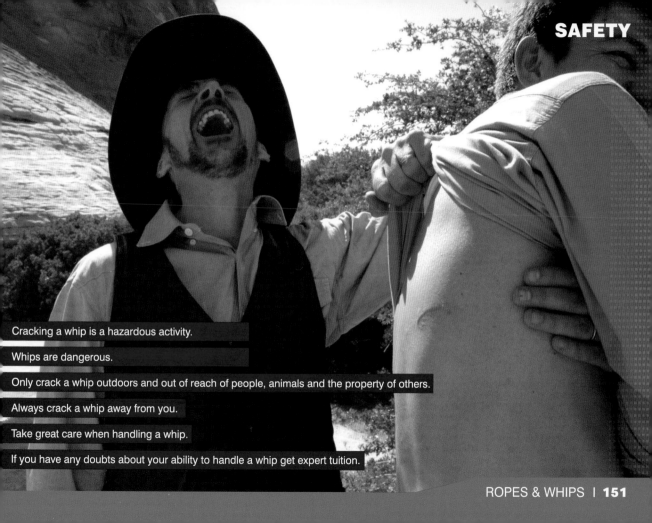

Cracking a whip is a hazardous activity.

Whips are dangerous.

Only crack a whip outdoors and out of reach of people, animals and the property of others.

Always crack a whip away from you.

Take great care when handling a whip.

If you have any doubts about your ability to handle a whip get expert tuition.

# SKATE

## SANDRO DIAS

SÃO PAULO, BRAZIL

154. **SAFETY**

156. **OLLIE**

158. **KICK** FLIP

160. **HEEL** FLIP

162. **SHOVE** IT

164. **UNTITLED**

# SAFETY

Skateboarding is a hazardous sport. The tricks that you are about to watch are carried out by an expert.

Always wear - a helmet, knee guards, and elbow pads.

Do not attempt any advanced skills before mastering the basics.

Always skate in a safe area away from traffic and pedestrians. Wherever possible, use a designated area.

Always consider your own safety and the safety of others.

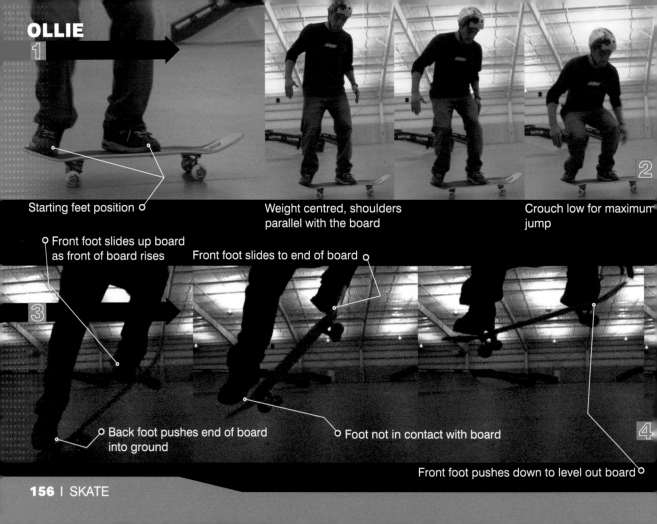

# OLLIE

**1**

Starting feet position

Weight centred, shoulders parallel with the board

Crouch low for maximum jump

**2**

**3**

Front foot slides up board as front of board rises

Front foot slides to end of board

Back foot pushes end of board into ground

Foot not in contact with board

**4**

Front foot pushes down to level out board

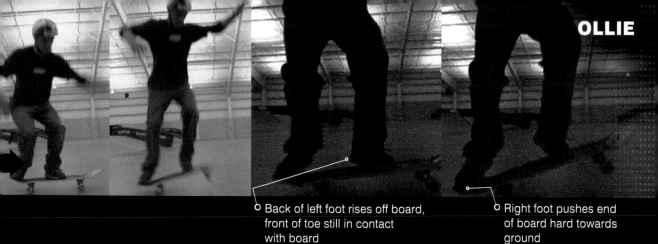

Back of left foot rises off board, front of toe still in contact with board

Right foot pushes end of board hard towards ground

NOTE: Keep weight balanced over board throughout Ollie.

# KICK FLIP

Toes of both feet approximately in middle of board, heels over side

Push down and slide forward as in an Ollie

Flick front foot off heel side of board, to flick it round

# EASIER WITH SPEED!

Balanced landing with both feet contacting board at same time, often the back foot lands first but if so the front foot should not be far behind.

Feet position

Front foot slides off front
toe side

Legs widen to move out of way of board

Land feet together, keep weight centred on board, lean back to compensate for natural forward tilt

NOTE: Stationary heel flip harder then moving heel flip.

to free deck

Back foot kicks behind
body to spin board

Front foot lands back on board first

Back foot lands in approximate starting position

# UNTITLED

Hit edge of board with tip of foot

A fraction before deck hits ground begin to pull foot back

Foot out of way

Practise balancing board o
by placing it on your foot

# BLADE
## FABIOLA DA SILVA
SÃO PAULO, BRAZIL

168. **SAFETY**

170. **BASICS**

174. **RAMP** BASICS

175. **DROPPING** IN

176. **JUMPS**

178. **GRINDS**

181. **RAILS**

SAFETY

No helmet!

BUSTED!

No pads!

Roller blading is a hazardous sport.

Always wear your helmet, wrist guards and knee pads - in some parks it is an offence not to wear such protective clothing.

Always warm up/ stretch before you skate in order to help avoid injury.

Before you start skating, try standing on grass in order to get your balance and the feel of the skates.

Learn the basic skills before you skate in a public place.

Learn how to slow down and stop - skating if you cannot stop is very dangerous for you and other people.

If you doubt your ability to copy the tricks accurately and safely you should not attempt them until you have sufficient skill.

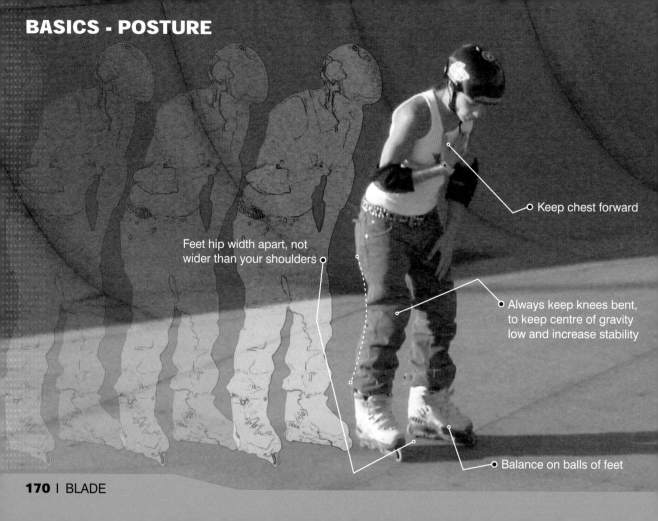

# BASICS - POSTURE

Keep chest forward

Feet hip width apart, not wider than your shoulders

Always keep knees bent, to keep centre of gravity low and increase stability

Balance on balls of feet

Use arms for additional balance

Push out and back for momentum

At mid-point of push, centre of balance just inside standing leg

# BASICS - BACKWARDS

Look over shoulder to see where you are heading

Keep chest forward

Keep knees bent

Skates cross over to create momentum

Guide movement with standing skate

Push skate away from body to create momentum

# RAMP BASICS

Keep chest forward

Keep weight on right leg if right-legged

Keep knees bent

Push down and up, away from ramp to 'pump' transition for momentum

Always start learning from the bottom of the ramp - do not begin by dropping in!! Learn how to ride ramp first.

## METHOD 1

• Keep knees bent, very important, it will keep you safe

ep chest forward

One skate locked onto coping between anti-rockers

## METHOD 2

Lock both skates on coping and then bend knees. Lean forward and drop in

Lean gently forward and drop in - if you gently lean forward as if to touch your toes the momentum will make you drop in.

Warning jumping is very dangerous

Always perform under professional supervision and wear all protective clothing

Make sure you have enough speed for jump - kick up legs as you lift off and keep skates together

When landing keep knees bent and chest forward to minimise impact on knees and body

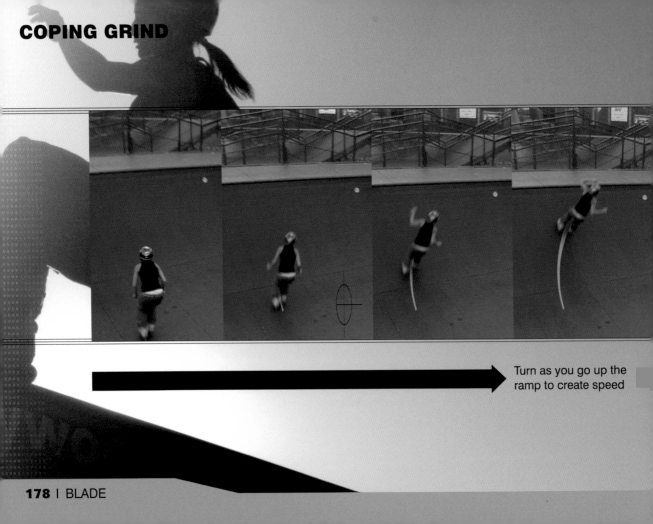

Turn as you go up the ramp to create speed

Land both feet on coping as in back stall disaster

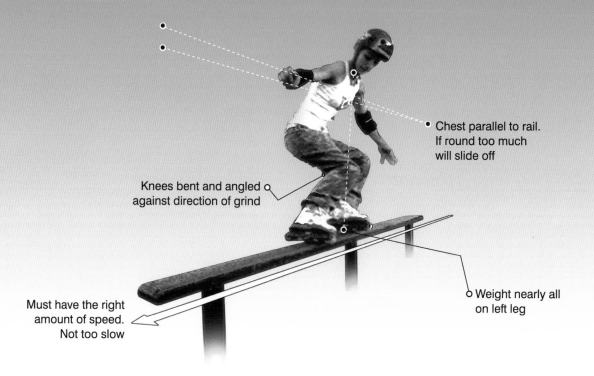

Chest parallel to rail.
If round too much
will slide off

Knees bent and angled
against direction of grind

Must have the right
amount of speed.
Not too slow

Weight nearly all
on left leg

# CARDS & MAGIC
## ALADIN
LONDON, UK

CARD

THROWS

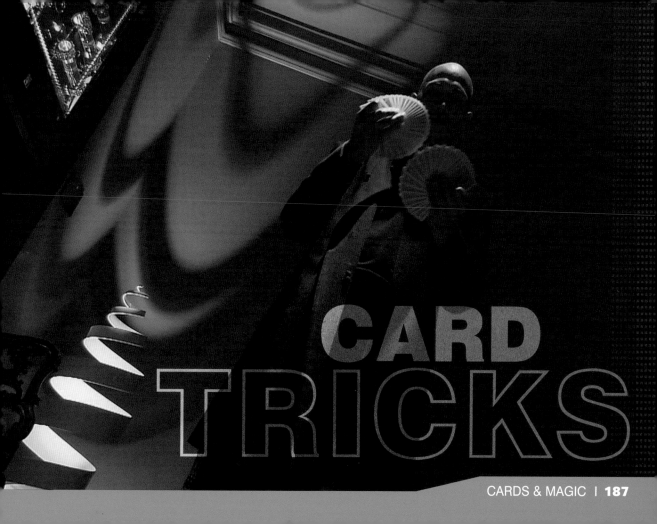

# CARD TRICKS

# BOOMERANGS

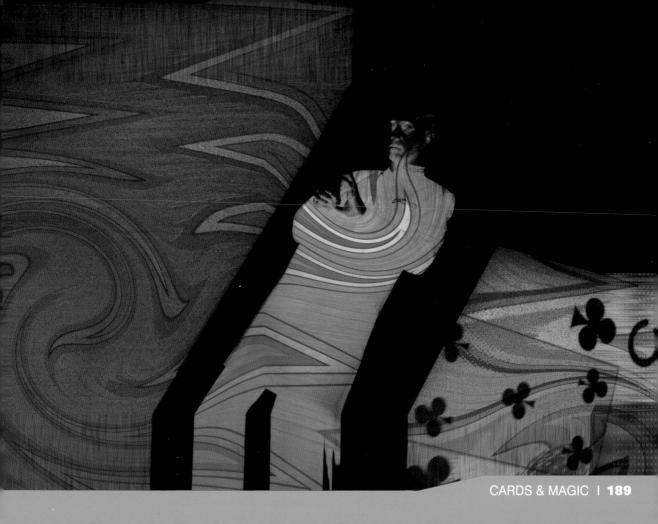

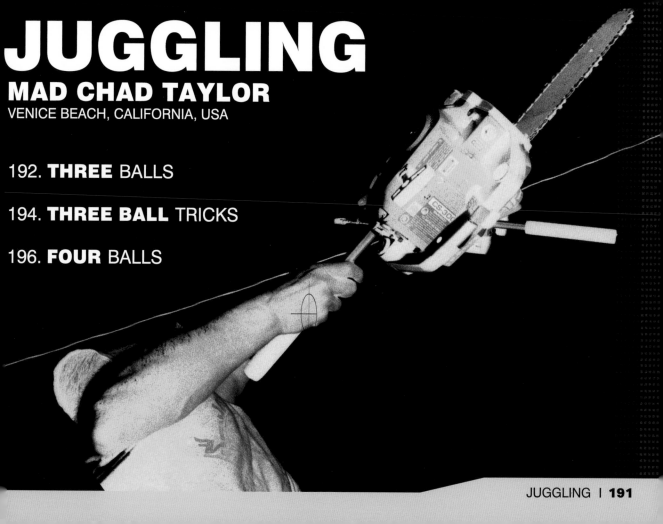

# JUGGLING
## MAD CHAD TAYLOR
VENICE BEACH, CALIFORNIA, USA

192. **THREE** BALLS

194. **THREE BALL** TRICKS

196. **FOUR** BALLS

# SAFETY

Mad Chad is a professional juggler - you are not Mad Chad!

Never juggle with chainsaws or any other sharp or hazardous objects.

Only juggle with safe objects that reduce the risk of harming you or others around you.

Always consider your own safety and the safety of others around you before attempting any trick.

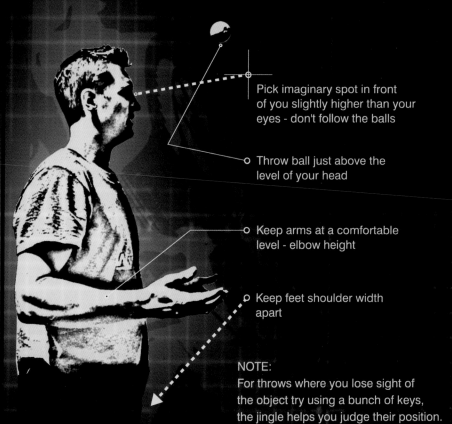

Pick imaginary spot in front of you slightly higher than your eyes - don't follow the balls

Throw ball just above the level of your head

Keep arms at a comfortable level - elbow height

Keep feet shoulder width apart

NOTE:
For throws where you lose sight of the object try using a bunch of keys, the jingle helps you judge their position.

THE **JUGGLING** PATTERN

# THREE BALL TRICKS

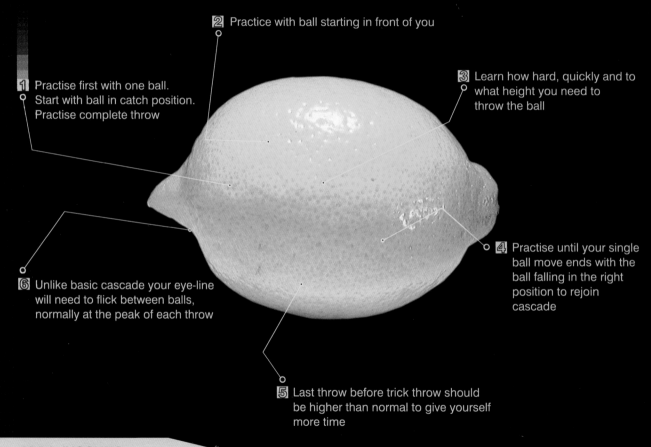

**2** Practice with ball starting in front of you

**3** Learn how hard, quickly and to what height you need to throw the ball

**1** Practise first with one ball. Start with ball in catch position. Practise complete throw

**6** Unlike basic cascade your eye-line will need to flick between balls, normally at the peak of each throw

**4** Practise until your single ball move ends with the ball falling in the right position to rejoin cascade

**5** Last throw before trick throw should be higher than normal to give yourself more time

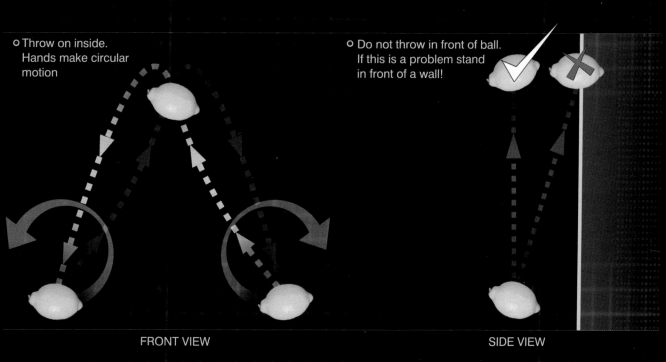

o Throw on inside.
Hands make circular
motion

o Do not throw in front of ball.
If this is a problem stand
in front of a wall!

FRONT VIEW

SIDE VIEW

NOTE:
Use a heavy object i.e. orange, lemon, beani bag etc - not tennis balls as they will bounce out of your hand.

# FOUR BALLS

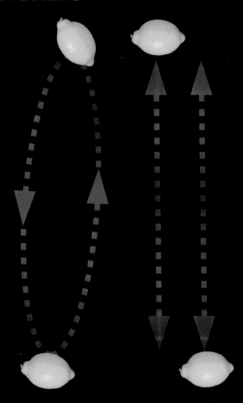

○ Learn with dominant hand first

○ Throw either in to out or columns next to each other

○ Throws should be higher than in a three ball cascade

○ When you can juggle two balls in each hand then begin juggling them at the same time. It may be easier to begin the first throw with your non-dominant hand

# FLATLAND BIKE

## MARTTI KUOPPA
HELSINKI, FINLAND

200. **SAFETY**

**FRONT WHEEL HOPPING**

202. BASICS

204. GETTING IN

206. GETTING OUT

208. **TAIL** WHIP

# SAFETY

- ○ Freestyle flatland is a hazardous sport.
- ○ You must wear all your protective clothing and equipment; helmet, elbow pads, knee pads, shin and wrist guards.
- ○ Martti is an expert who has mastered his bike - you are not Martti.
- ○ Take professional tuition before attempting any of these skills.
- ○ Practise in a safe place - away from cars, people and water.

# FRONT WHEEL HOPPING
## BASICS

NOTE: This is the first and key step to learning your balance for flatland

1 Reverse bars

2 Hold brake in with two fingers only

3 Place right foot on peg

4 Head should be forward of handle bars to maintain balance

You should be able to do this for as long as you want before progressing to the next trick

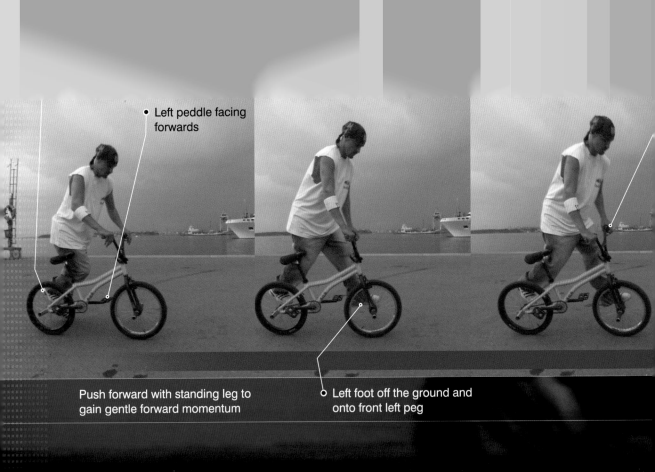

Left peddle facing forwards

Push forward with standing leg to gain gentle forward momentum

Left foot off the ground and onto front left peg

Right foot moves to front right peg

HOP!

# FRONT WHEEL HOPPING
## GETTING OUT OF IT

Rotate handle bars through hopping

Place right foot on frame •

• When wheel rotates 45°
lift right leg from peg

Continue to rotate front wheel •

• Place left foot on pedal and ride away

# TAIL WHIP

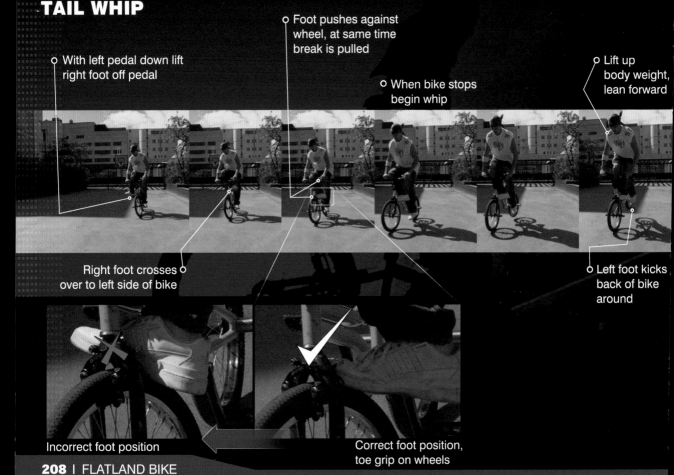

With left pedal down lift right foot off pedal

Foot pushes against wheel, at same time break is pulled

When bike stops begin whip

Lift up body weight, lean forward

Right foot crosses over to left side of bike

Left foot kicks back of bike around

Incorrect foot position

Correct foot position, toe grip on wheels

As kick ends arms rotate to continue whip

Land foot back across top of frame against seat bar

Left foot moves back

Right foot onto right pedal and away

# RUGBYKICKS

## CARLOS SPENCER

AUCKLAND, NEW ZEALAND

214. **PUNT**

216. **UP** & **UNDER**

218. **FLOATER**

220. **DROP** KICK

222. **BANANA**

224. **JOHNSY**

# PUNT

Eye-line fixed on ball

Eye-line fixed on point of contact

Hold ball vertically

Kick here

Kick with this part of foot

KICK PROFILE

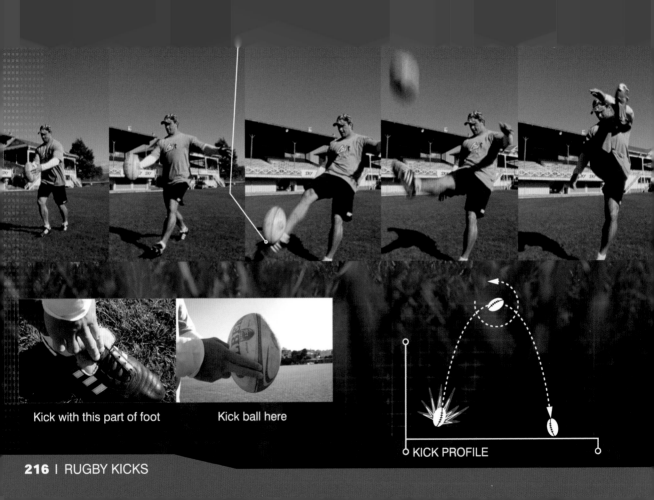

Kick with this part of foot

Kick ball here

KICK PROFILE

# FLOATER

Kick this part of ball

One-handed horizontal release

Kick with this part of foot

KICK PROFILE

# DROP KICK

Hold ball vertically

Kick with this part of foot

Kick near bottom of ball

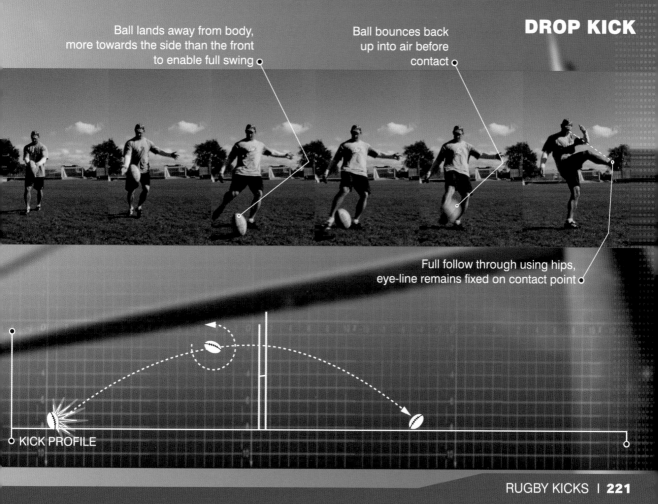

**DROP KICK**

Ball lands away from body, more towards the side than the front to enable full swing

Ball bounces back up into air before contact

Full follow through using hips, eye-line remains fixed on contact point

KICK PROFILE

# BANANA

Kick this part of ball

Kick with this part of foot

# BANANA

Not full follow-through

TOP VIEW

The Banana - shorter than the punt - arc curves sideways

The Punt

KICK PROFILE

# JOHNSY

Hold the ball horizontally

Kick the bottom edge of the ball

Kick with this part of foot

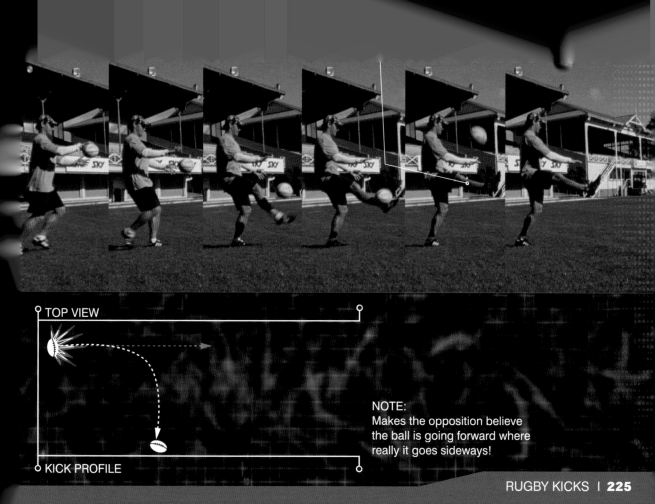

TOP VIEW

KICK PROFILE

NOTE:
Makes the opposition believe
the ball is going forward where
really it goes sideways!

# GOLF
## VICENTE BALLESTEROS
PEDRENA, SPAIN

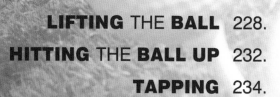

**LIFTING** THE **BALL**  228.

**HITTING** THE **BALL UP**  232.

**TAPPING**  234.

# LIFTING THE BALL
## PART 01

Position toe of club (sand wedge) under the ball

Ball will initially roll towards the middle of the club face

Initial lift created only with wrist movement

Move wrist only

As ball and club come forward there is a slight raising of the forearm

When club face clears front of body then arm begins to move forward

Ball back in stance

# SLOW & FLUID ACTION

Heel of club away from you - club flat to the ground

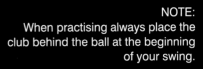

**HIT DOWN WITH THE HEEL FLAT AND PULL THE CLUB BACK UNDER THE BALL**

# TAPPING

Simply pull club head up and down while keeping it level

Easier with a sand wedge

Club hits ball at approx. same height each time, do not chase the ball

Keep club head level at all times

# BAR FLAIRING

## CHRISTIAN DELPECH

BUENOS AIRES, ARGENTINA

238. **SAFETY**

240. SHAKER **BEHIND BACK**

242. SHAKER **BEHIND HEAD**

244. SHAKER **HAND TO HAND**

246. SHAKER **SPINS**

250. **SPIN** CATCHES

252. **LONG** POUR

254. **STALL**

256. **BEER**

262. **ICE**

263. **SWORD & CHERRY**

# SAFETY

Bar flairing is a hazardous activity and should be carried out with extreme caution.

For all bottle skills, practise with plastic bottles outside in a safe environment.

Glass can kill.

In bars where barmen flair - they always! have rubber matting on the floor, and even this does not prevent breakages.

Be very careful and aware of those around you.

## TAKE CARE WHEN YOU FLAIR!

# SHAKER BEHIND THE BACK

Grip top of shaker with end of fingers and thumb

When hand level with top of head begin release of shaker

Shaker continues to rise to above head level

Eyeline focused on shaker

Sight still fixed on shaker

Begin to move arm and shoulder out of the way by twisting hips

Catching hand open and
ready to catch

# SHAKER BEHIND THE HEAD

Shaker hand rises as catching hand begins to move behind head

Release shaker approx. at this point

At point of throw forearm close to right angle

Hand in position to receive shaker

Eyes track path of shaker

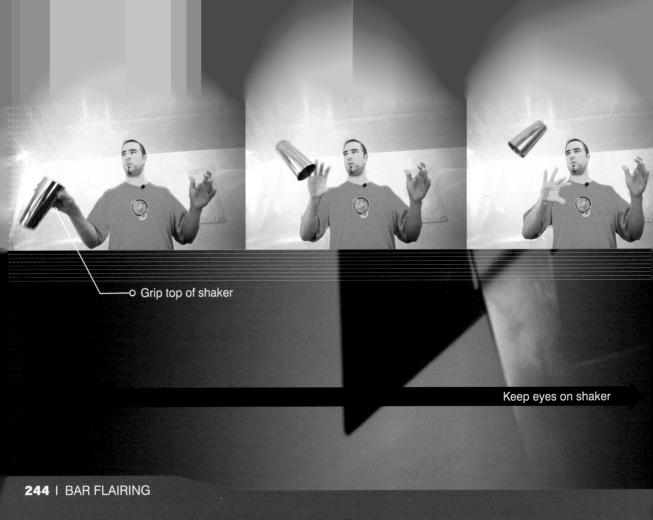

Grip top of shaker

Keep eyes on shaker

For two spins, throw slightly higher than for one spin

# SHAKER SPINS
## PALM SPIN - PART 01

Spin **shaker** on this part of **palm**.
Place **shaker** on palm, spin **with other**
hand **to find** natural balance **point**

Arm movement helps create momentum for spin,
when beginning start with shaker parallel to body

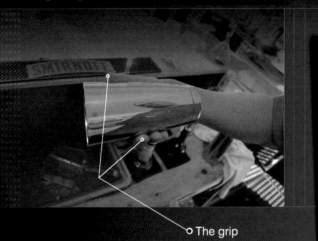

o The grip

o Keep thumb and fingers bent back
out of way of shaker when spinning

Just one spin

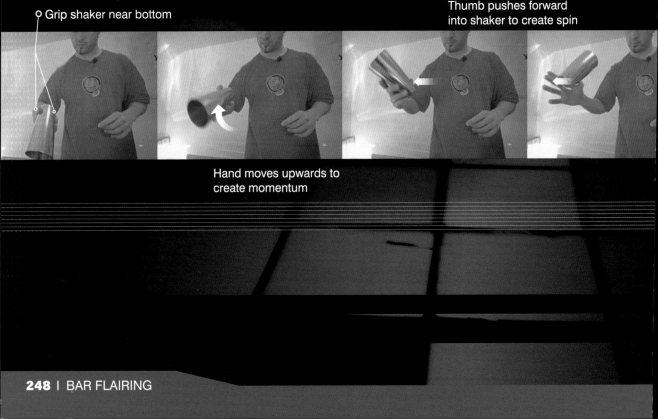

Grip shaker near bottom

Thumb pushes forward
into shaker to create spin

Hand moves upwards to
create momentum

One spin to catch

BAR FLAIR

Practise to get the momentum right to create a single rotation between throw and catch.

Throwing hand should hold top of item.

Try to catch bottles by neck as this enables further spin throws and pours.

In bars where barmen flair - they always! have rubber matting.

pour starts, more visual

maximum height

Shaker drops, bottle stays in **same** position

When shaker in bottom position raise bottle slightly for increased power

Bring shaker and drop bott to end pour

Find natural balance point on hand - it varies from person to person

- Stall by bringing hand downwards with bottle to gently cushion it to a stop.
- Adjust angle of hand to maintain balance.
- Practise by holding bottle by neck with two fingers then lifting it straight up and stalling it with same hand.
- You can learn this in one day - guaranteed.

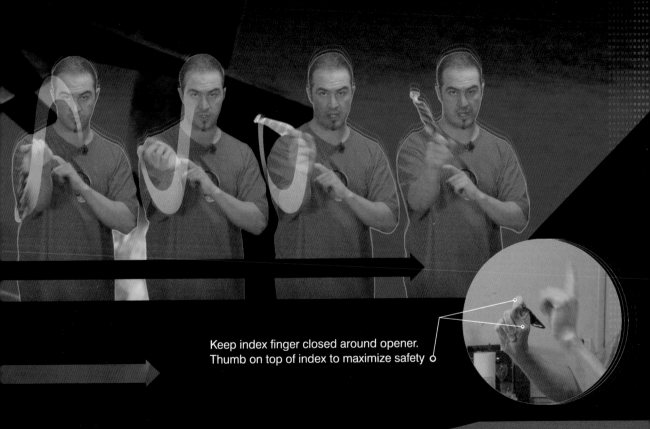

Keep index finger closed around opener.
Thumb on top of index to maximize safety

Close thumb around bottom of opener to secure it against bottle neck

against lid

Middle fingers closed around opener

Keep pinky above bottom lip of beer top to prevent bleeding

PULL!

Hand with opener comes over the top of beer bottle which results in opener facing downwards out of palm, ready to hit falling top.

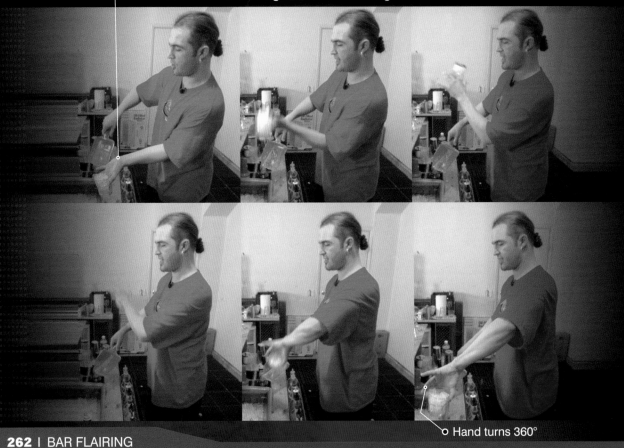

ICE

Hold glass with arm turned over and palm out.
This enables fast enough turn to hold ice in glass

Hand turns 360°

Keep **eye**-line focused on cherry, position **s**word under path of falling cherry

Get a jar of cherries and practise. It's sticky but it's very powerful. You can use pitted olives as well as cherries

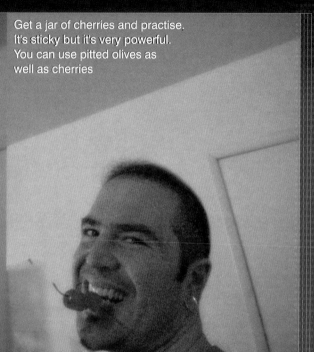

Keep head tilted backwards so that sword points straight up in the air

Grip very tightly between teeth. The cocktail sword or cocktail stick should be straight up not at an angle

Accurate throws causing less head movement will increase the percentage of successful catches.

# POOL

## THORSTEN HOHMANN & MIKE MASSEY

FULDA, GERMANY & LOUDON COUNTY, USA

266. **BASICS**

270. **BREAKS**

274. **X-TREME** DRAW

275. **X-TREME** FOLLOW

276. **BANK** SHOTS

278. **INVERTED SPIN** BANK SHOT

280. **3 CUSHION** BANK SHOT

282. **JUMP** BANK

284. **MASSE** SHOT

286. **MASSE** JUMP

288. **MASSE** SWERVE

290. **FINGER** POOL

# BASICS
## THE BRIDGE - OPEN BRIDGE

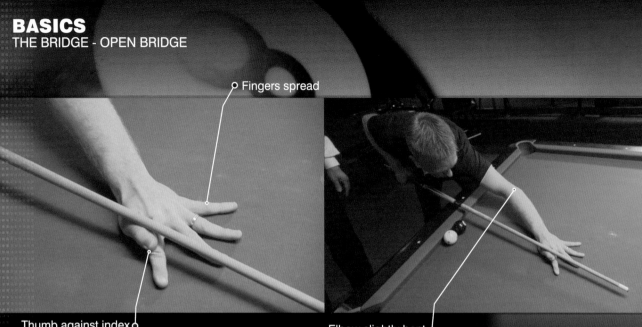

Fingers spread

Thumb against index

Elbow slightly bent

Cue height with the open bridge can be adjusted and kept <u>level</u> by spreading out or pulling in the fingers.

Elbow at right angle when tip just beyond fingers

Like holding a bird

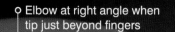

Thumb, index and middle fingers all touching

One hand's distance

Last point of focus is the target spot on the object ball. Like throwing a dart

Hips face approx. 45° away from cue for correct line-up - this can be worked out by holding the cue at its balance point and adjusting accordingly

- A clean cue and dry, clean hands reduce friction.
- Professionals predominantly use the closed bridge for American Pool.
- Nearly all use it for power shots.
- STAY DOWN AFTER SHOT - FAILING TO DO SO IS THE MOST COMMON MISTAKE OF ALL!

# BASICS
## CUE BALL CONTROL

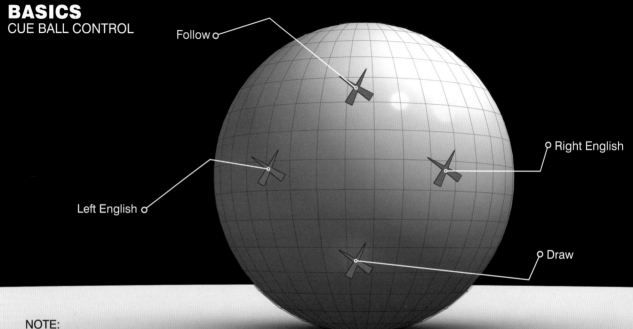

Follow

Right English

Left English

Draw

NOTE:
- English = Side

- Keep cue level - follow through

- To stop cue ball dead at impact, ball must be sliding when contact is made.
  The friction of the cloth will cause the ball to have natural follow-through after a certain distance depending on how much power and what spin has been applied to the ball.
  Therefore to stop the ball dead over a distance will require more draw and/or more power.

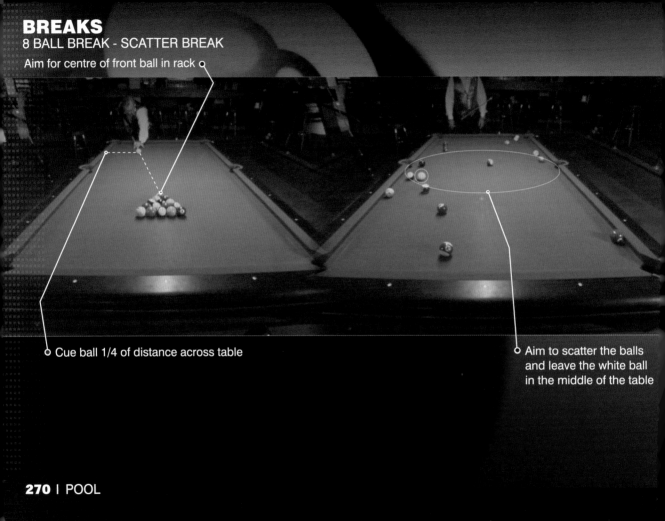

# BREAKS
## 8 BALL BREAK - SCATTER BREAK

Aim for centre of front ball in rack ○

○ Cue ball 1/4 of distance across table

○ Aim to scatter the balls and leave the white ball in the middle of the table

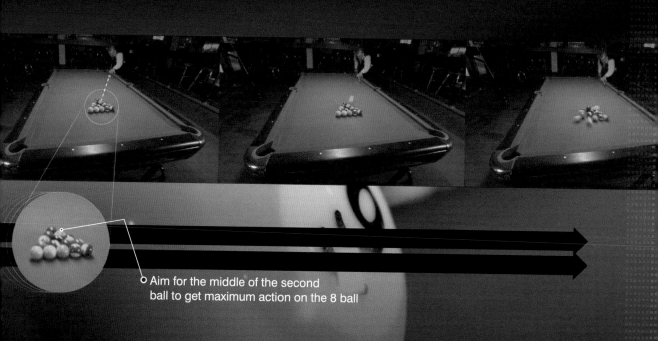

Aim for the middle of the second ball to get maximum action on the 8 ball

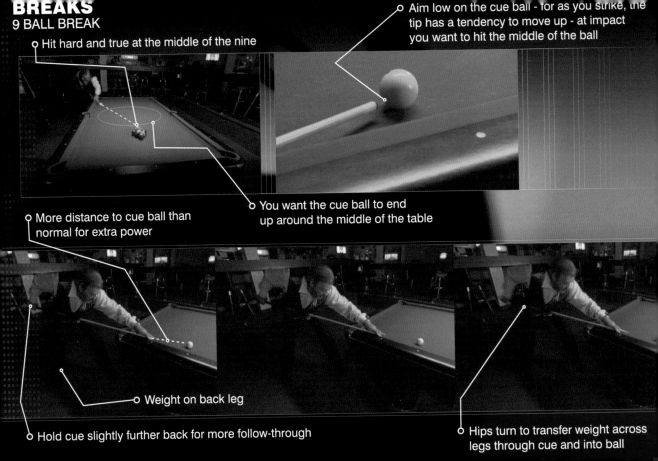

# BREAKS
## 9 BALL BREAK

Hit hard and true at the middle of the nine

Aim low on the cue ball - for as you strike, the tip has a tendency to move up - at impact you want to hit the middle of the ball

You want the cue ball to end up around the middle of the table

More distance to cue ball than normal for extra power

Weight on back leg

Hold cue slightly further back for more follow-through

Hips turn to transfer weight across legs through cue and into ball

NOTE:
If your opponent racks for himself make sure the balls are frozen!

Elbow drops to keep cue level
and insure maximum power
on follow-through

# X-TREME DRAW

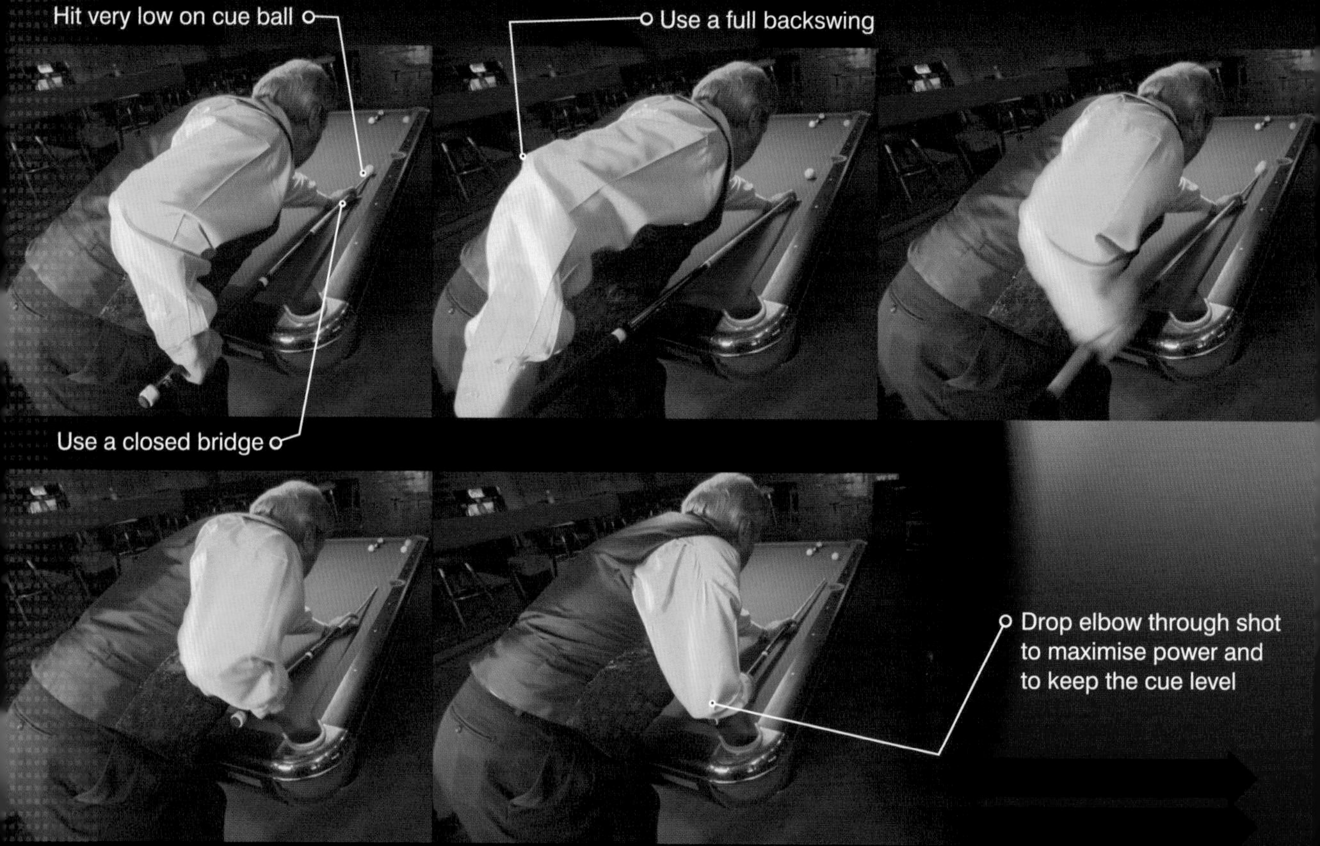
Hit very low on cue ball
Use a full backswing
Use a closed bridge
Drop elbow through shot to maximise power and to keep the cue level

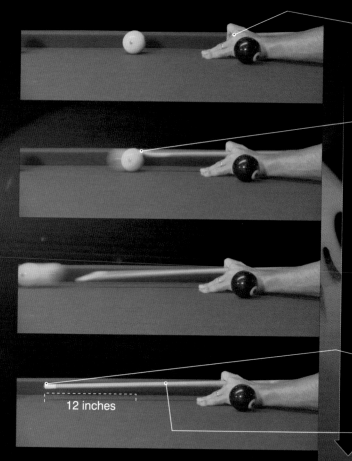

# X-TREME FOLLOW

○ Maximum pull back - cue tip at edge of bridge

○ Hit high on cue ball

○ Maximum follow-through used - approx. 12 inches

12 inches

○ Keep cue level through shot

FAST
SLOW

NOTE:
The harder you hit the ball the less of an angle it will rebound off the cushion.
Using side or cutting the ball will increase or decrease the rebound angle off the
cushion depending on which side you cut or impart spin.

# INVERTED SPIN BANK SHOT

NOTE:
Because the cue ball has made the 8 ball spin anti-clockwise it reverses off the cushion against its natural angle and rolls into the top corner pocket.

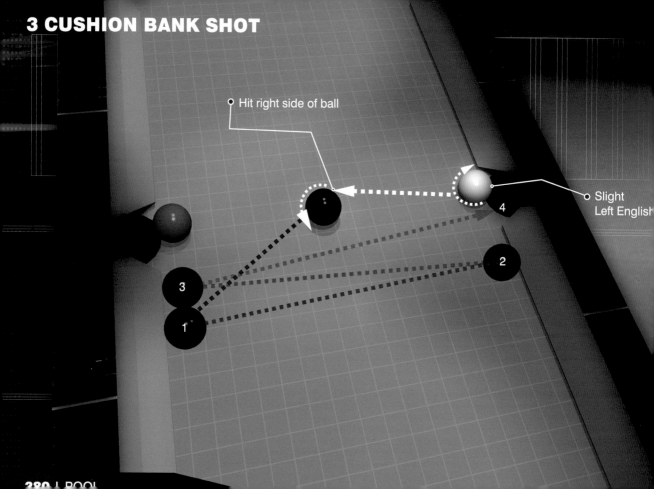

# 3 CUSHION BANK SHOT

Hit right side of ball

Slight Left English

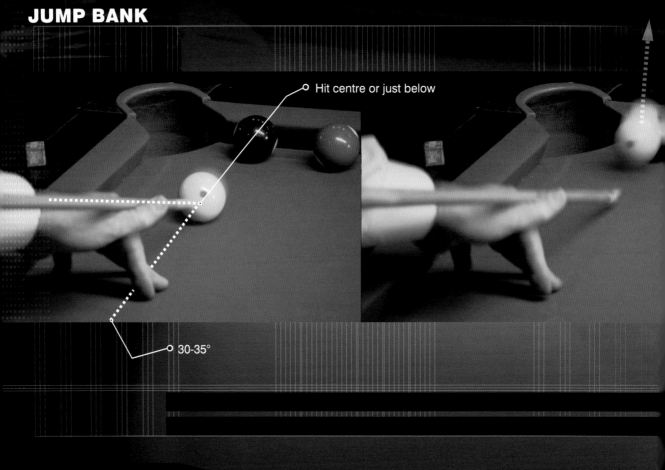

Hit centre or just below

30-35°

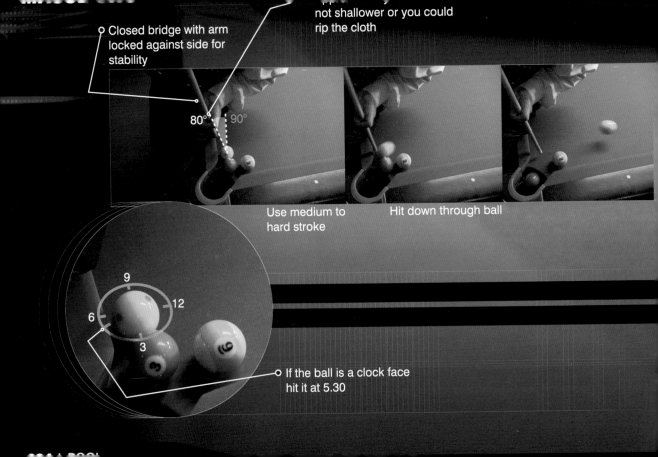

Closed bridge with arm locked against side for stability

not shallower or you could rip the cloth

80°  90°

Use medium to hard stroke

Hit down through ball

9
12
6
3
6
If the ball is a clock face hit it at 5.30

by Fast Eddie in the movie "The Hustler".

Hit ball in middle or 1/2 a cue tip beneath

Cue angle mirror
ball leap angle

3
2
1

- The more vertical the angle of the cue the steeper the jump of the ball. The ball is driven into the table and therefore comes off at the opposite angle.

- For a straight jump aim at the middle, or 1/2 a cue tip below middle of the ball as it faces you.

- For steeper jump shots a jump cue is often used and needed.

- For Masse swerve jump shots aim off centre in accordance with which way you want the ball to swerve after it lands.

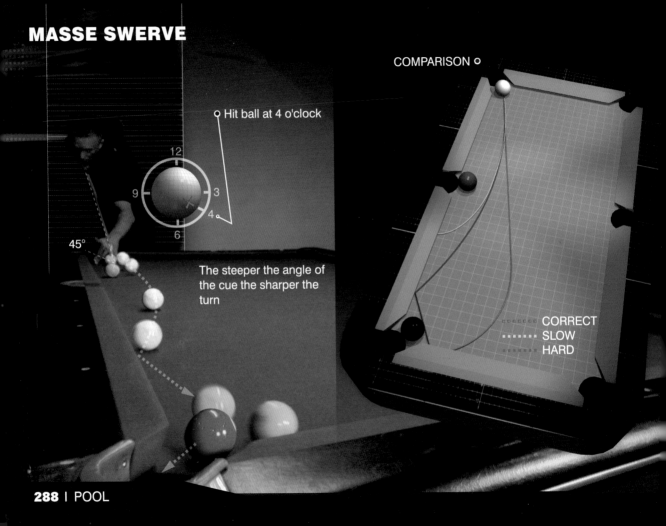

# MASSE SWERVE

COMPARISON ○

○ Hit ball at 4 o'clock

12
9 | 3
4 ○
6

45°

The steeper the angle of
the cue the sharper the
turn

CORRECT
SLOW
HARD

Increase elevation of cue to gain more swerve on ball

**NOTE:**
The normal mistake is to hit the ball too hard - the harder you hit the later it curves.

# FINGER POOL

Hold ball between thumb and middle finger, snap them together to make the ball spin

The angle of the hand, and thumb position will determine the direction the ball spins after release

NOTE: Practise away from windows, glass and children - the balls can fly from your hand off the table if you get it wrong!

# FOOTBAGBAG

## VASEK KLOUDE
PRAGUE, CZECH REPUBLIC

294. **BASIC** KICKS

296. **TOE** DELAY

298. **INSIDE** DELAY

300. **CLIPPER** DELAY

302. **DEXTERITY**

# BASIC KICKS

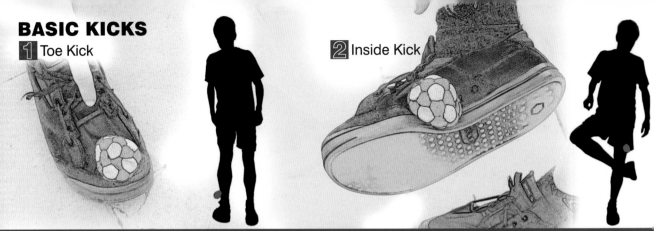

**1** Toe Kick

**2** Inside Kick

NOTE: Keep eyes focused on ball at all times.

**3** Outside Kick

**4** Knee Kick

# TOE DELAY

Catching foot rises to just below standing foot's knee level

Foot starts descent. knee starts to straighten

Foot skips up to begin momentum for delay

As standing foot completes skip, downward momentum continues through bending of the knee

Just after point of contact, catching leg stops straightening

**TOE DELAY**

Footbag is slowed down through the bending of the standing leg

# INSIDE DELAY

Side of foot parallel to ground

Higher point of contact than in toe delay

Standing foot is pointing slightly inwards after skip

Knee bends

Leg continues to straighten throughout delay

More pronounced skip with standing foot than other delays

Foot lands with hips turned to position catching foot under footbag

Legs work together to delay footbag

Foot pulls bag up

Rotation caused by knee movement, not thigh!

Bag continues to rise. Foot moves outwards to begin circle

Leg moves around front of bag

Toe delay

# MORE

**STREET** BIKE 306.

**BREAK**DANCING 308.

**BATON** 310.

**YO-YO** 312.

**SKATE** 314.

**SCOOTER** TRICKS 316.

# BYRON
# ANDERSON

SEE DVD FOR:
**BUNNY** HOP
**BAR SPIN** BUNNY HOP
**180°** TO **ROLL BACK** TO **FAKEY**
**MANUAL**

# **KRYPTO**KNIGHTS

**BREAKDANCING**

SEE DVD FOR:
**FLARES**
**POPPING**
**SIX** STEP
**HEAD** SPINS

BATON

AMYARELLANO

BATON

SEE DVD FOR:
FINGER **TWIRL**
FINGER **FLIP**
THUMB **FLIP** & **TOSS**
ARM **ROLL**

# BILL DE BOISBLANC

SEE DVD FOR:
**HOPS**
**WIND** UPS
**LOOPS**
**UNTWISTING**
**ROUND** THE **WORLD**
**TWO** HANDS

SKATE

NO
SKATEBOARDING
LAMC 602 P.C.

# DEREK'S
# SKATE SHOP

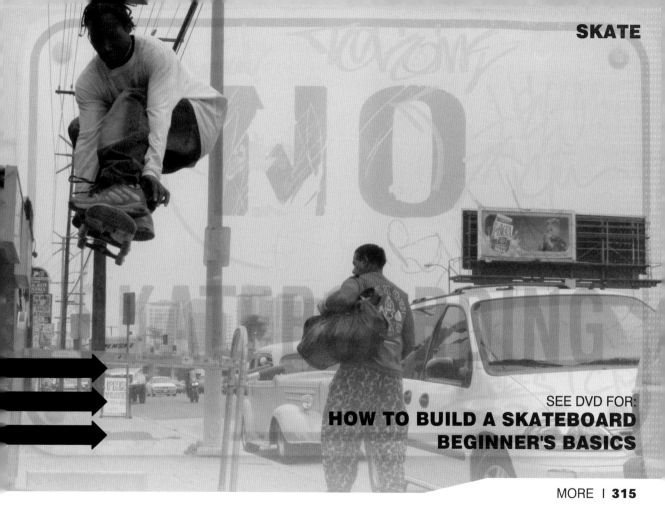

SKATE

SEE DVD FOR:
**HOW TO BUILD A SKATEBOARD
BEGINNER'S BASICS**

# SCOOTER TRICKS

SEE DVD FOR:

**OLLIE**
**TAIL** WHIP
**MANUAL**
**360°**
**BAR** SPIN
**DOUBLE** TAIL **WHIP**

# RAZOR
# SCOOTERS

THANKS TO

ADAM REES ADRIAN ROWBOTHAM ALEXANDER CORBETT
CONRAD WITHEY DAN BAILIE DAVID CLARK DEXTER
FERGUS REES GEORGIE PINN GILDA REES
GUY WALSH HUGO DE GROOT JOHN MILLS JULIAN GILMORE LOGAN
MACDOUGAL POPE MAREK ANTONIAK MARK
ALLEN MARK BANKS NEVILLE SHULMAN NICOLA
CORMACK PETER HODGES SALLY SHERATT SEBASTIAN
BELCHER SOFIA PALEOLOGO STEVE WEINTZ
TED LERNER VIJAY BADRI SPACE DESIGN LTD
GAVIN CROSSWELL WARREN EVANS KAREN HARKNESS
SPIRAL MUSIC CLIFF OVENDEN JOE CRISP ON SIGHT
FOR HD CAMERA AND ON LINE SERVICES TONY MAHER
ANDY LEE THE MILL POST PRODUCTION BUMBLE DAVIS
JAMES BAMFORD KAI VAN BEERS 24-7 DVD YIVES REED MATT
GOBLE U.S FILM SERVICES: GOOD FOOT FILMS PETER
BERGLUND LORRAINE BERGLUND MATT
STENERSON CASINO GAMING SCHOOLS OF NEVADA
NICK KALLOS THAMESDOWN SOFTWARE FULFILMENT
LTD JOE FOX CHRIS MASUY PHIL HOWELLS MATHEW
ROSNER ADAM GLEN MATTHEW DURKAN ALAN SKIDMORE
AXIS FILMS ALLEN THOMAS ALADIN GEOFFREY WANDSELL

THIS IS NOT THE END